An inspiring thought
held captive
by a reluctant pen
inspires no one.

This book is dedicated to my loving family and friends, and countless others, who have blessed me over the years with their kindness and support. Thank you.

LOOKING BACK AND RUNNING FORWARD

DISCOVERING WHAT IT
MEANS TO BE BROKEN

HEIDI KINNEY

Copyright © 2021 Heidi Kinney
http://heidikinney.com

ALL RIGHTS RESERVED. No part of this book may be reproduced, stored in a retrieval system, distributed, or transmitted in any form or by any means, including photocopying, recording, or other electronic or mechanical methods, without prior written permission of the copyright owner except for the use of brief quotations in a book review. For permission requests, contact heidi@heidikinney.com.

Scripture quotations are from The ESV® Bible (The Holy Bible, English Standard Version®), copyright © 2001 by Crossway, a publishing ministry of Good News Publishers. Used by permission. All rights reserved.

ISBN 978-1-7372557-0-3

This book is a memoir. The events described are true to the best of the author's memory. The author assumes no responsibility or liability on behalf of the consumer of this material. This book is not intended to be a substitute for medical or professional advice on any issue, physical, psychological, or spiritual. The author in no way represents or endorses any company, corporation, or brand, mentioned herein. Any perceived slight of any individual or organization is unintentional.

Cover designed by MiblArt.

Table of Contents

Introduction 1
1. Depression 101 5
2. Shaking in my Bed 15
3. Not Just a Headache 22
4. Running Down Charles Street 26
5. You Can't Get There from Here 29
6. Treatment Begins 33
7. California Dreaming 37
8. Killing Cancer 40
9. Back to Counseling 44
10. A Lonely Wedding Day 48
11. Saved by Grace 54
12. Answered Prayer 59
13. Becoming a Mother 64
14. Building a Distraction 68
15. Surprise! You're Not Sterile 72
16. Eat, Vomit, Repeat 74
17. Appointment Day 78
18. Google Desperation 82
19. A Man Becomes a Child 87
20. Camping and a Kennedy 92
21. Writing for my Beloved 99
22. Widow Etiquette 112
23. 911 Again 115
24. The Twenty-Dollar Bill 118
25. Permission to Destroy 121
26. The Merry Helpers 124
27. No More School 133
28. A Mom and her Backhoe 137
29. The Widow's Curse 141
30. Shrinking into Nothingness 145
31. A Cookout Casualty 150

32. A Bible Study Revelation	154
33. Escaping the System	159
34. Selling My Security	163
35. Leaving Our Church	175
36. The Forty-Dollar Salad	179
37. Afraid to Run	189
38. Running Forward	195
39. A Beautiful Tomorrow	202
40. Freedom from Fairy Tales	208

Introduction

Dreams can inspire, and dreams can frighten. Sometimes a dream can do both at the same time. Many years ago when I was constantly struggling with my endless responsibilities and questioning my place in the world, I had an inspiring and frightening dream. It was inspiring in that it prompted the writing of this book, and frightening because the writing forced me to face and expose my inner self in a way that was uncomfortable and painful.

Although the details of the dream are now hazy, there are several key elements that I remember. In the dream, I was standing in the middle of a room surrounded by familiar people. All at once, the people disappeared, and I was alone in the room. I felt confused and afraid. Then the emptiness left, and I sensed three people were there with me even though I could not see them. I did not know who they were, but one of them spoke to me in what I perceived to be a male voice. He spoke with perfect clarity and without emotion. "Have you written your testimony?" is all he said.

Instead of answering the question directly, I uttered a

list of excuses. I can't recall what I said, but it was as if I was telling the questioner how awful my life was and using that as a justification for why I hadn't written my testimony. Ignoring my response and in the same direct manner as before, the voice repeated the question. Again I rambled off my list of reasons. I can't recall what happened next in the dream, but I remember waking up wondering whether the dream was a message from God. It was so clear and so perplexing.

In the days leading up to the dream, I had been praying intently for direction. I had been feeling lost for a long time, and I was desperate for guidance. Was this God's answer? Was I supposed to write my testimony?

So much time has passed since I had that dream, that I can't recall when I even had it. Having almost convinced myself that it was meaningless, I ignored it for a long time. After a while, a nagging sense that it may have been an answer to my prayer crept in. This feeling continued to grow stronger until I could no longer ignore it. I thought about my testimony. What was my testimony? I had absolutely no idea, but I began writing anyway.

My writing would start, and then it would stop. I could never seem to find the right words. This happened so many times I wondered whether I even had a testimony. I didn't have what some people call a mountaintop experience, and I didn't feel like I had made it to the other side of anything worth writing about. After all, I was still struggling daily. How could I write a testimony?

After several years I finally made some progress when I realized I was living out my testimony every day. My testimony was not a onetime event but a continual collection of moments. My story was my testimony, and I could look back and write about pieces of that story, at least the pieces that I still remembered.

Over the past two decades, I have encountered many trials, twists, and turns. Along the way I have neglected to reflect on the remarkable road on which I've traveled. Dealing with the day-to-day events as they come, I give little thought to what happened yesterday, last month, last year, or last decade.

It isn't until I face a memento of an earlier time, usually found while searching for a present-day need, that I realize that I did once exist in another reality. That reality contained people and circumstances that are no longer present today. It is in these moments of confrontation with an earlier existence that I am forced to question myself. Am I the same girl today that I was then? Who was that girl anyway?

Sometimes when I find things, I try hard to look back. Often, I don't even recognize my previous self. What was I thinking about then, and why was I thinking it? Trauma is a mysterious beast. It manifests itself in so many ways, affecting the body and mind. Memory loss is one of these manifestations.

There are portions of my past that I can't recall. I've found souvenirs that should suggest to me a picture of a past event. Sometimes, as hard as I try, I just can't quite see that picture. It's like trying to tune the dial on an old television, and all you see is a fuzzy screen with intermittent images of the program. You can almost see it, but then it's gone. Or you imagine that you almost see something there because you know in your mind that you're supposed to be seeing something. It is your past, after all.

Introduction

Sometimes, I don't look back at all because it is just too painful. In looking back, I must face my past. It is often easier to just try to forget. I am good at forgetting. I have blacked out sizeable chunks of my life. It is sad when I think about it. The mind copes with situations in strange ways.

However, I think there is a difference between forgetting and choosing to forget. If I purposefully choose to forget, instead of remember the person I was, I will never truly appreciate or be grateful for the person I've become. God has carried me on a tremendous journey so far. How can I not embrace that journey and be thankful for it, for all of it?

So what follows is my response to the question posed in that unusual dream. It is my testimony, my story. All I can recall of the past are bits and pieces, and not all the details are clear anymore. However, I will trust there is a greater purpose at work for sharing what I can remember. Perhaps these memories will inspire you or, at the very least, take you somewhere else for a little while. My prayer is that sharing my story will bless you in some way.

CHAPTER 1

Depression 101

Feeling awkward and nervous, I naively and far too eagerly accepted my diagnosis. Timidly, I answered the mental health counselor's questions. To an unsuspecting observer, I was a healthy young woman employed as a secondary mathematics teacher, the dream job I had trained so hard for and convinced myself was right for me. I should have been happy, but something was wrong.

This wasn't the first time I had been in counseling, or even the second. In high school, my mom had persuaded me and my sister to visit a counselor. I can't recall why, or if this was before, during, or after the divorce. All I remember is that I hated it.

During that initial visit as a teenager, the therapist had quickly labeled me as someone who ran away from trouble instead of dealing with it. By assigning this label, he implied something was wrong with me. I didn't like confrontation, true, but I didn't agree that I was running away from anything. What was there for me to deal with? My parents' divorce was out of my control, and sitting around discussing it with a stranger seemed pointless to my teenage brain. Maybe it made more sense to my sister, because she returned for more sessions. The only session I remember is that first one, and I didn't appreciate being labeled. I had always been labeled.

Growing up, I never understood why folks insisted on calling me shy or quiet. Perhaps they didn't think it was offensive to assign a label to a child. It was. That they felt the need to say anything at all showed that something was wrong with me—at least that's how I perceived it. Would they have preferred that I was aggressive and loud? It was not in my introverted nature. Besides, I had been raised with a belief that children should be seen and not heard. If I was quiet, then I couldn't upset anyone or call attention to myself. Content to be in the background, that was me. I was not supposed to speak up or be in the spotlight. I accepted that truth and lived by it. Over time, my label acted as a shield. In the presence of strangers or people who made me uncomfortable, I could hide behind my label. As a shy, quiet person, I didn't have to talk, because no one expected me to say anything.

However, I wasn't always quiet. When at ease, I could be chatty. In high school, my best friend and I would talk for hours. Other times, we would sing. I fondly recall the two of us hanging out in her bedroom watching Disney movies. We knew the words to every song in *The Little Mermaid* and would sing them with gusto. I can only imagine what her parents sitting in the other room thought of our silliness.

Watching these films, the fairy tales enraptured me. Maybe my parents didn't have a great relationship, but surely my prince was out there, and someday he would find me and I would be rescued. Even when my world became unstable, my belief in happy endings held firm. I wanted the fairy tale desperately.

Was I running away from things when I would sleep at my friend's house? No. I think I was just being a typical teenage girl who would rather spend time with a friend than listen to an argument at home. According to the therapist I was running away. I had something wrong with me. I was defective.

In college I had my second counseling experience. I was living on campus in a freshman dorm and enjoying a new sense of freedom when one of my roommates introduced me to a guy that she'd befriended. He was unlike anyone I'd ever met before, a cute surfer from New Jersey, with an easygoing style and an intoxicating smile, who often rode around campus on his skateboard. Completely smitten, I ignored my better judgment about him. He was a popular guy with lots of female friends, and I'd heard rumors about a brief relationship he'd had with another freshman girl. This should have been a warning sign, but I ignored it. Rumors were not reliable. Besides, I was in college now, and there were different rules. I didn't have to be the same shy girl that I was in high school.

So I let my attraction for him show, and before long we were a couple. Maybe he would be my prince. I was surprised that someone attractive and popular liked me. Although I'd had a few boyfriends in high school, those relationships were not healthy. I usually dated guys just because they asked me out and then continued the relationships for the wrong reasons. I enjoyed feeling liked, even when the feeling wasn't mutual. My self-esteem was low, and having a boyfriend made me feel better.

Being the girlfriend of someone that I was infatuated with was something new. Thinking I couldn't possibly be worthy enough to keep his affection, I did everything I could to keep the relationship going. I thought I could control it, could control him. I inserted myself in his affairs as much as possible. He couldn't stray if I was always there. He enjoyed being around his friends, but I never felt comfortable in the group. My introverted self was clueless in social situations, and I had no conversation skills. The more I tried to stay in his business, the more anxious and overwhelmed I became. Despite my anxiety, we enjoyed many happy months together. He even hinted about getting married after college.

A year into our relationship, one of his female "friends" became friendlier. Unable to cope with the demands of school, work-study, a disgruntled roommate, and the new competition for my boyfriend's affections, my behavior became erratic. I would call his dorm room repeatedly when I knew he didn't have classes, just to check if he was there. Sometimes I would go looking for him. One time I noticed his car parked outside the dorm where the female friend lived. So I parked my car near it and went for a walk, all the while hoping he would notice my car and go looking for me. My behavior was at its worst the day he invited me to go with him and his friends to visit another friend out of town. I never should have gone. I felt out of place and my boyfriend ignored me. At one point the group went for a walk and I hid in my boyfriend's car, convinced that I wasn't wanted. No one came looking for me. I cried and may have even screamed. I felt trapped. I wanted to leave but I didn't know where I was or how I could get back to campus. I didn't have a phone. All I could do was stay in the car and wait. I don't know if anyone saw my meltdown but eventually the group returned, and we drove back to school. My boyfriend broke up with me shortly after this incident. I was crushed.

A kind friend at school helped me after the breakup. She knew I was struggling emotionally, and suggested I visit the school's counseling center. Reluctant to see a counselor because of my previous experience in high school, I initially dismissed the suggestion. Upon further prompting, I gave it a chance. I can't recall how often I went to counseling, but it was more than once. I eventually stopped going, moved on with my life, and tried to forget about the surfer.

Fast forward to my early twenties, and my life consisted of getting up early, driving for an hour, teaching all day, driving for another hour, coming home, chatting briefly with my mom, going to bed, getting up for dinner, preparing for my next day's classes, and then going back to bed again. I was sleeping way too much, and I knew something was wrong. On weekdays, sleeping was my favorite escape from the world.

I found myself back at yet another counselor's office. This counselor was about my age, which made the situation even more awkward, as I think we were both living out our first "real" jobs. She was kind and seemed happy with her career choice. I was withdrawn and miserable.

Thankfully, most weekends were different because I had a fun boyfriend who enjoyed being active. If I could catch him before he was off with his friends or off to work on yet another project, we would spend time together.

Often, we spent time together while he worked on his projects. Sometimes he would work on his house, truck, or Jeep. Other times he would build or repair things for others. He had many skills and enjoyed putting them to use.

My boyfriend, Rob, and I met during the summer that followed the breakup with the surfer. I had been single for several months and emotionally healthy. Summer had reunited me with my best friend from high school, and we'd enjoyed going out dancing at clubs and having drinks with other friends. It was on one of these summer nights that I met Rob. He was a friend of a friend that my best friend was speaking with one evening. He invited us to join them at a party, and we went. That one decision changed my life entirely.

Rob was an attractive and quiet guy. Love at first sight is not how I would describe our first encounter, because he was intoxicated—very intoxicated. All I remember about him that night was that he was calm and sweet. Until that point in my life, I'd thought drunk men were all loud and mean. His contrary demeanor mystified me.

Throughout that summer, my best friend and I spent time with Rob and his friends. Over time, this led to a relationship. Rob was unlike anyone I had dated before. He was a hardworking, smart, honest, independent, fun, and lovable guy with a core group of friends and a close family that regularly spent time together. He didn't seem to mind that I was quiet and socially awkward.

He lived with his mother, his older brother, and one of his three older sisters. His father had died when he was little. Rob had decided not to pursue college. Instead, he worked full time in HVAC and had ambitions of owning his own company and rental property. We were on somewhat divergent paths, but it didn't matter. It was summer, and we were enjoying ourselves with little expectations.

With Rob, I was an unfamiliar person, an adventurous person. We would ride his watercraft or go hiking in the mountains. Sometimes we would just travel somewhere new and explore an antique store or look at old houses. We both loved historic architecture and vintage items. He often challenged me to do things I'd never done before or ever thought about doing, like wakeboarding and mountain biking, and it was fun.

That summer romance never ended, and we continued to see each other. Even though I went back to school in the fall, we called each other during the week and saw each other most weekends. Sometimes we would drink too much when his friends were around. Rob and his buddies liked to party, but it didn't seem out of control, and I didn't think much about it. School and work always took priority over partying.

My mom had always stressed the importance of hard work and a college education. Financially, our family had lived on a tight budget. I grew up cutting coupons and shopping from the discount racks. Despite our circumstances, my mom would tell me and my sister repeatedly that we would go to college someday, and we believed her. My sister and I both worked hard to maintain honor-roll status in high school, and we each were accepted to our chosen colleges. Student financial aid, scholarships, and parent loans allowed us to attend. There was no way that I would mess up my college education by acting irresponsibly.

Rob had goals too, and he took steps to reach them. He purchased a foreclosed multifamily rental property and began restoring it. At some point, he even left his full-time job to work for himself. Often, our time together would involve me coming to his rental property. He was always working on something. I didn't mind though, because I had fallen in love and just being with him made me happy. This relationship was unique. I wasn't anxious about retaining his love, and I didn't like him just because he liked me. We loved each other and enjoyed spending time together.

After graduating from college, I spent the summer babysitting Rob's adorable new niece and searching for a teaching job. We continued to see each other as much as possible. After several job interviews at various schools, I was offered a mathematics teaching position at a private school within driving distance. I gratefully accepted the job and began teaching that fall.

All was well for many months. I adjusted to my new schedule and looked forward to spending time on the weekends with Rob or with other friends when I wasn't preparing for my classes or correcting papers. I poured myself into being the best teacher I could be. I enjoyed creating unique lessons for my students and interacting with them each day. My class load was heavy, but I gave it my all.

At some point I became overwhelmed. It got so bad that thinking about taking a nap after work was the only thing that got me up in the morning. I knew I needed help. So I was back at a counselor's office.

After I had answered her questions, the counselor determined that I had unresolved issues from my childhood and was suffering from depression. Alas, I had a diagnosis that seemed to make sense. I had taken psychology courses, and the counselor's explanation correlated with what I had studied. Sure, I had issues from my past. That must be it! I was a textbook case. I was broken.

After the first counseling session, I returned for many more. Over time I became embarrassed that I needed to be there. I didn't like that something was wrong with me. As we worked through role-playing to encourage verbal communication skills, which I detested, and discussed the possibility of adding an antidepressant, I felt my world slipping away. I didn't want to be depressed, but I was not happy.

Agreeing to medication was my first mistake. This meant that besides counseling, I had regular visits to a psychiatrist since the counselor could not prescribe medication. I struggled with side effects and the constant changes in dosages and medications to find something that would supposedly work. Surely I was broken, and medication would fix me.

Mistake number two was the decision to move in with Rob. We had been seeing each other for several years and moving in together seemed like a logical next step. Of course, I thought marriage was the most logical next step, but he was not ready for that. I don't think it was the desire to move in with him that primarily drove my decision, but the desire to move out of my mom's home to become a "real" adult. With student loans and the low salary that I earned teaching at a private school, I couldn't afford to pay for an apartment and living expenses on my own. Sharing expenses made moving out a possibility.

By this time Rob had almost finished renovating his rental property and had a vacant apartment. He wanted to move out of his mom's home too. Moving into the rental property together seemed ideal. Instead of paying rent, we agreed that I would pay for the utilities, groceries, and some other bills. The plan appeared to make sense.

Besides, I was certain that living together was just a precursor to getting engaged and then married. I had found my prince. Certainly, he would propose soon. Sure, we would live together without being married, but that didn't seem completely wrong. People did it all the time. There was a part of me that felt like it was wrong to live together before marriage, but it was a small part and easily ignored. I needed a change, something to look forward to, and this was my chance. I did not know then how wrong I was.

CHAPTER 2

Shaking in my Bed

Surprised at how comfortable my seat was, I tried to relax as I stared out the window. I could get used to this. Riding a commuter bus back and forth to Boston each day wouldn't be so bad. It was only about an hour each way. Somehow, riding on that bus with other commuters, I felt more like a grown-up than I ever had before, and I was finally excited about my life. It was the first day at my new dream job, and I was optimistic that it would be great. At least, I was optimistic until our bus entered the city.

Commuting into the city was new to me, and I wasn't sure how to do it. Although I was excited, I was nervous. My commute would involve a bus ride, a subway ride, and then a walk to the office building. I had wanted to do a dress rehearsal of sorts days earlier by pretending that I was commuting to work and following the steps I needed to get to the building. Since I wasn't confident that I could do it on my own, I had asked Rob to come with me. He declined, so I told myself that I didn't need to do it. I was wrong.

I didn't realize that the bus made multiple stops. So when a sizeable group of passengers rose to get off the bus, I got off with them. I assumed they would walk toward the subway and that I could follow them. Instead, they immediately dispersed in different directions.

Looking around, I saw no sign of the subway and didn't recognize any landmarks. I did not know which way to go. Yes, I should have asked the bus driver before getting off the bus. I didn't ask questions back then. That was not me. Instead, I just kept quiet, determined to figure it out on my own.

Not knowing what to do, I started walking. The subway couldn't be too far. I had been in the city many times before, and subway stations seemed to be everywhere. However, that was in another part of the city. Geographically, I had no idea how far that area was from where I was standing now. Surely there had to be a subway station nearby.

I walked some more, but I couldn't find the subway. I panicked when I realized the clock was ticking. It was frighteningly close to the time I had been told to arrive at my new job. I had taken an early bus, which should have allowed for plenty of time to get there had I gotten off at the right location. Now, I would be late on my first day!

I considered hailing a taxi, but I wasn't sure how to do that. Besides, I didn't even have a phone to call one and doubted whether I had enough money to pay for the ride. Should I just turn around and go home? How could I even do that? The bus terminal was at the subway station, and I didn't know how to get there!

With tears building, I kept walking. Why couldn't Rob have just gone on a test run with me? Was that too much to ask? Why didn't I force myself to do it alone? Why didn't I just ask the bus driver where to go? Why did anxiety always overtake my common sense? I was finally hired for the job I wanted, and I had ruined it on my first day. Why did I think life was getting better?

Living with Rob had proven to be a poor decision. It was a tremendous strain on us both financially and emotionally. We were young and foolish. Although we thought we were making wise decisions, we weren't. We purchased new furniture on credit and spent money instead of saving. Everyday bills were more than I thought they would be, and money was always tight.

Rob was still partying with his friends regularly. I had lost interest in that and was hoping marriage and settling down was on the near horizon, even though part of me suspected that it wasn't. I didn't initially let those doubts stop me from dreaming about a fairy-tale wedding and creating a beautiful binder full of ideas and plans. Ironically, I was living a fairy tale in the pages of that wedding binder because Rob was not ready for marriage, and even though I refused to admit it, neither was I.

Not too long after moving in together, my mood slipped again. The realization that living with Rob was not working coupled with frustration from my teaching job was too much. I wasn't sleeping all the time like before, but I just wasn't happy. Over time, teaching had become a source of stress. I loved working with my students, but I found it difficult to interact with other teachers. The social requirements caused me anxiety, and coworker politics confused me. I didn't fit in. Convinced that teaching was not for me, I pursued other career options. Since writing had always been a passion I explored options in that field.

Thinking education was the first step to pursue

anything new, I completed some graduate classes in writing and publishing. Before I had barely begun my classes, I became convinced that I belonged in publishing and that I could find a new dream job. At the end of my second year of teaching mathematics, I left my job, certain that I was on the path to finding my true calling.

I still needed an income to pay the bills, so I spent the summer working as a temporary employee for several companies through a nearby temp agency. Fortunately, the agency provided ample data entry and clerical assignments to keep me busy. Interestingly, I was making more money temping than I had while teaching.

During my nonworking hours, I continually applied for jobs in the publishing field. I thought that if I just kept applying that I would find something quickly. I was wrong. Even though I had several interviews, none of them were fruitful. As the summer ended, I felt like I had a decision to make: continue temporary employment while looking for what had now become an elusive job, or go back to teaching. Begrudgingly, I applied for some teaching positions. and a local school hired me.

Even though I was relieved to have a full-time job again, I was still not content. I continued to apply for jobs in the publishing field. By the fall of the following year, I found success at last when an educational publisher in Boston offered me a position as a mathematics editor. It was a six-month contract position with the possibility of renewal. The insecurity of the job didn't matter. I finally had a position in my desired field, and it thrilled me. It was the first thing I had looked forward to in a long time.

I don't know how long it took me to find the subway on that first day of my new publishing job, but I did eventually find it. Once I did, I easily navigated to the stop near the office building. Walking as quickly as I could, I wondered if I would still have a job once I got there. Maybe they would change their minds. What kind of employee shows up late on her very first day on the job?

Thankfully, my new boss's secretary was a kind woman and was gracious to me when I arrived. Relieved that I had finally made it there and grateful that I still had the job, I got to work. Finally, life was looking up, or so I thought.

After several months at my new job, my boss asked me to attend a conference with some other editors. One perk that I'd enjoyed while teaching for the private school was when they would send me to a conference or workshop. I loved learning fresh ideas. So I was excited about this conference opportunity.

However, my excitement turned to fright the night before the conference. Fast asleep, a sudden violent shaking of our bed woke me. I thought it was a train. Our apartment had train tracks right behind it, and sometimes it felt like the building shook when trains passed. It took me a few minutes to realize that it wasn't a train—it was Rob shaking uncontrollably in the bed. Although this had never happened before, I suspected he was having a seizure.

Though it lasted only a short time, it felt like time stood still. Half asleep and frozen with fear, I stared at Rob. Then it was over. He immediately went back to sleep. I didn't know what to do and panicked. Should I wake him up? Should I call an ambulance? What had just happened anyway?

So I did the only thing that I knew how to do at that

moment. I called my mother, and she calmed me down. After the call, I woke Rob up and attempted to explain what had happened. He didn't remember any of it and didn't want to listen to me. He wanted to go back to sleep and refused to go anywhere. I spent the rest of the night lying awake by his side, watching him sleep because I was paranoid it would happen again.

By morning I was able to reason with him. His mouth was sore from biting the inside during the seizure, so he now believed that something had happened. I convinced him he should go to the hospital.

I didn't know what to do. I wanted to go with him, but I was headed to the conference that morning and had no way to get in touch with my coworker, who I was supposed to pick up and drive to the conference. Should I stand her up and go to the hospital with Rob? Would she be stranded all day? Would I be jeopardizing my new job if I skipped the conference? Some of my superiors would be there.

(Ironically, years later, I would face a similar dilemma that would force me to choose between Rob and my career again.) Rob going to the hospital alone was out of the question. What if it happened again while Rob was driving? Thankfully, we contacted my brother-in-law, and he offered to help.

The conference was a blur. I was there, but I wasn't. I couldn't focus during the sessions because I couldn't stop worrying about Rob. I wanted to be with him. Was he alright? Was choosing to attend the conference the right decision? Hours went by before I received a phone call from my brother-in-law telling me they were back from the hospital and that Rob was fine. Adult-onset epilepsy was the diagnosis, and lifelong medication was the proposed treatment. I had many questions, but Rob didn't have answers. He accepted his diagnosis and life went on.

CHAPTER 3

Not Just a Headache

Sitting in a little cubicle with my head down and my eyes focused, I was busy editing a manuscript. Occasionally, I would look up to check my email. It was a typical workday morning, until it wasn't.

For several days prior, Rob had experienced headaches. He wasn't one to suffer from prolonged headaches, so this was new. Having grown up suffering from migraines, headaches were not a cause for alarm in my mind. Headaches were not serious. Just take some acetaminophen and lie down in a dark, quiet place until it passed. That was what usually worked for me.

His headaches were different. This morning the pain had gotten so bad that he went to the emergency room at a local hospital.

I don't recall if I had even spoken with Rob that morning. Although we were still a couple, by this time we were no longer living together. His partying had gotten out of control. Even though we had purchased furniture together and behaved like a married couple, we were no closer to getting engaged than when we'd first moved in together. Rob was not ready, and my ideas about a fairy-tale wedding did little to persuade him.

Even though Rob knew that drinking alcohol could interact with his seizure medication, he did not refrain from drinking. Spending time with his friends took precedence over our relationship, and his friends liked to drink. Rob could have resisted, but he didn't. That was not his style.

We had struggled financially. My editing job provided a slightly better income than teaching, but I had added commuting expenses. Rob had purchased a second multifamily rental property and had several loans to pay each month. He was still trying to get his HVAC business going, but he had to spend much of his time working for others to maintain a regular income. Although he would never admit it, he needed the income from the rental space we were occupying.

So when I was finally ready to admit that moving out was the only option that would spark a much-needed change, I rented an apartment and he moved in with some friends. This was a big test for our relationship. Would we remain as a couple or separate? We would call each other during the week and see each other most weekends. We loved each other, but we were both still growing into ourselves.

After living alone in an apartment for several months and then living several more with a roommate who didn't like to pay her share of the bills, I pursued homeownership. I completed a first-time home-buyer's course and took on part-time jobs to supplement my income. Meanwhile, Rob was working hard at establishing his business while maintaining his rental property.

Living apart, our relationship gradually grew stronger.

We both focused on improving ourselves, and this led to more quality time together. I was no longer in counseling or taking medication and was feeling well emotionally. After I had saved enough money for a house deposit, I began looking for a property and eventually found a small fixer-upper in a quiet town nearby. It was a short drive to the train station from which I could commute to and from work. This house is where I was living and where I had commuted from on that typical workday morning when I received the news about Rob.

At first I learned that Rob had gone to the same local hospital that he had visited after his seizure. Not long after, I was informed that a helicopter would be airlifting him from the local hospital to a hospital in Boston. This news and the seriousness of what it meant didn't sink in until I told a coworker friend and saw the look of shock on her face. It was then that I realized that this was dreadful news. Being airlifted meant it was a serious emergency, not just a terrible headache.

Since I was already in Boston, I made plans to meet one of Rob's sisters at a subway station and go to the hospital with her. My coworker friend generously escorted me to the subway station and gave me directions on how to walk from the subway stop to the hospital. My knowledge of how to get around the city had improved, but I had never been in the hospital area.

The hospital was terrifying. I stood in a small, uncomfortable room with Rob's siblings and his mother. Panic lingered heavily in the air as we waited for someone to tell us what was happening with Rob.

After what seemed like a very long time, someone came in to speak with us. I stood there in utter shock when we were told that Rob had a lemon-sized mass on his brain. I had no idea what that meant, but I knew it was serious, and I suspected Rob would not be leaving the hospital that day.

CHAPTER 4

Running Down Charles Street

There I was, sitting at my desk again at work, when the phone rang. Several days had passed since the airlift, and Rob was still in the hospital. What seemed to be an emergency now seemed like a waiting game. Rob's family and I still didn't know what was going on. None of the doctors had provided any details about his diagnosis or plans for treatment.

I answered the phone to hear a frightened Rob on the other end. I could tell from the quiver in his voice that he had been crying, and I did my best to calm him down. Rob didn't cry. He was a guy who kept things in. His friends used to joke that he was like a rock. Maybe it was a stone. But he seldom showed extreme emotion of any kind. He was a happy, easygoing guy. Hearing his voice shake, I knew something was very wrong.

He told me that some doctors had finally come to see him and given him some information about his condition. He wouldn't tell me what they said, but he asked me to come immediately to see him. I assured him I would. That meant leaving work, again. I didn't have any meetings that day, so my time was flexible. I could just stay late, I reasoned with myself. Most likely no one would notice if I took an early lunch. I headed out the door as fast and as stealthily as I could.

Since the subway was not a direct route and it would take more time, I went on foot. Between the day of the airlift and this day, I had figured out how to walk to the hospital. It was a lengthy walk, but I'd throw on my commuting sneakers and head to the hospital after work each day. This day, though, once I left my office building, my fast walk turned into a run.

Seeing someone dressed in office attire racing toward a subway station at popular commuting times was common in Boston. However, I wasn't near a subway station, and it was late morning. As fast as I could make myself go, I ran down the narrow sidewalks of Charles Street, an upscale area of boutique shops. I didn't care if I looked odd. I had to get there quickly. Rob needed me.

Maneuvering in and out of pedestrians and carefully treading the slippery winter streets and sidewalks, I pushed myself to keep running. I was still getting used to walking quickly while commuting, so my fitness level was low. Running was not something I did.

Sweating, out of breath, disheveled, and heart racing, I arrived at the hospital in record time. Rob would be happy. I had gotten there quickly after his call to comfort him.

Opening the door to his hospital room, I gasped at what I saw—one of his sisters sat by his side. I couldn't believe it! Had he known she was coming? Had she called him that morning or told him the night before? Had he called her? Why had I just risked my job by racing there to comfort him? Rob sat there calmly, as if nothing had happened that morning.

After a few minutes of awkwardness, she left the room so I could visit with him alone. He didn't seem to understand what the doctors had told him. Or maybe he didn't want to tell me. This might have been when he found out he would need surgery. What I remember is that I didn't stay long. I had to get back to work before someone noticed that I was missing. Besides, I felt like he didn't need me there anymore.

CHAPTER 5

You Can't Get There from Here

Driving to Boston scared me. The traffic was relentless with drivers frequently zigzagging between lanes like they were avoiding obstacles in a video game. You had to be hyper alert at all times. I did not like it, and I didn't do it. Sure, I worked in Boston and traveled in and out of the city every day, but I didn't drive to the city. I rode the commuter rail or subway and then walked wherever I needed to go. Even so, I only knew a small part of the city. I knew how to get to work from the train station and vice versa. I knew how to get to my favorite lunchtime spots, like the sandwich shop and the park benches near the water at Boston Common, and I knew how to get to several nearby subway stations. I also knew how to get to the hospital from my office building, but I didn't know the geography of the entire city.

Knowing how to navigate only a portion of the city on foot gave me some reservations about driving. Plus, I did not do well in traffic. I don't remember why I deviated from my normal commute by driving on this day. I just know I was going to the hospital to spend time with Rob, and I drove there.

Anxiety and anticipation filled me. I successfully made it through the traffic into the city. Rounding a bend, I saw the hospital. All I had to do was get to it. This was when my trouble started. I could see it, but I couldn't get to it. How do I get to it?

The road was like a highway, with several lanes of traffic on opposite sides and a barrier in between. The hospital was on the opposite side of the barrier, and there were no exits, at least that I could see. Surrounded by aggressive drivers who all seemed to know where they were going, I became anxious and confused. How do I get to the hospital?

Forced to keep driving, to move along with the rush of vehicles on all sides of me, I passed the hospital. My mind panicked. I did not know where I was going or how to get back to the hospital. The panic soon manifested into screaming, which turned into sobbing. Why did I think I could do this? My eyes became so flooded with tears that I could barely see the road. Overwhelmed, a strange idea filled me. Maybe I should take my hands off the wheel. I had reached my limit. I had not slept or eaten much of anything in days. Stress and worry consumed me.

Besides worrying about Rob, I was concerned about losing my job. I had taken time off from work to be at the hospital, and I was making up the time as best as I could by going in early and staying late. My brain was exhausted. During an editorial team planning meeting at work one day, I closed my eyes for a second and fell asleep sitting there. I didn't know if anyone noticed since the meeting continued after I awoke, like it never happened. Maybe they were too shocked to say anything. Maybe my supervisor had reported the incident.

To top it all off, my boss had invited me to attend a regional conference. The company was paying for flights and lodging for me and a few others to attend the multi-day event—a tremendous opportunity. I was still a contract employee, having had my contract renewed several times. Taking part in this conference could have led to a promotion. I'd been all set to go until Rob's hospitalization.

The situation was eerily familiar to the one when Rob had his first seizure years earlier. Again, I had to decide between Rob and my job, but this time it was much more serious. Going to the conference would mean I would be away for his surgery. How could I do that? How could I leave the man that I loved when he was about to have brain surgery?

So even though my company had already arranged the details of the trip and purchased the airfare, and even though I knew I was risking my career, I backed out of the trip. I was scarcely keeping my act together, and on this day, all I had wanted was to drive to the hospital to see Rob. Since I couldn't even do that successfully, maybe I should just let go of the wheel.

Sobbing hysterically, I fought with myself as I struggled to hold on. But how could I let go? How could I do that to Rob? No, I had to keep going.

The next thing I remember is sitting in my car at a gas station. I don't know how I got there. Now away from the traffic, I was able to calm down. After composing myself, I asked someone at the gas station for directions to the hospital, and navigated there without incident.

Although I told Rob I had trouble getting to the hospital that day, I didn't give him specifics, and I never told him I almost gave up. He didn't need to know about that. He was fighting for his life, and he needed me to be strong. I didn't know then just how strong I would need to be or where that strength would come from.

CHAPTER 6

Treatment Begins

Sitting around what felt like an enormous table, Rob's family and I waited for the doctor to speak with us about Rob's prognosis. His mother, siblings, and most of their spouses were present. Not being related, I felt like the oddball out. When the doctor came in, a family member introduced everyone. I was introduced to the doctor as Rob's fiancée. I tried to correct whoever said it, but someone else backed it up.

What was going on? Had I missed something? Why was everyone suddenly referring to me as Rob's fiancée? Maybe they were trying to legitimize my place at the table. Perhaps a fiancée held more standing in situations like this than a girlfriend. Sure, we had recently discussed the possibility of getting married, and Rob had even asked about styles of rings, but we were not engaged. He had not proposed. We had dated for so long that I wasn't sure when and if our marriage would ever happen.

Distracted and confused by my new title, I tried to understand the doctor when he spoke. He was a neuro-oncologist. I didn't even know what that meant. Then came the announcement of the suspected diagnosis, which the surgery would later confirm: stage four glioblastoma. The doctor told us that stage four was the highest of the stages. It was bad, really bad. Rob had an aggressive, incurable, malignant brain tumor.

I was in shock and disbelief as the doctor continued in his monotone voice, rambling off statistics and the general prognosis. He said that most people with this tumor type live less than five years. I refused to accept it. None of it made sense. Rob didn't fit any of the statistics. He was young and healthy. How could he have a brain tumor?

What was even more confusing was that he had been seeing a neurologist for years for his supposed adult-onset epilepsy. Had he had a tumor all this time? The neuro-oncologist explained that Rob would need surgery, radiation, and chemotherapy. Having had no experience with any of these, I didn't know what to expect, but I would soon find out.

Before the surgery, Rob had some decisions to make. Living with roommates that worked all day and partied on the weekends would not provide an optimal environment for someone recovering from brain surgery and undergoing cancer treatment. Besides that, Rob could no longer work full time, if at all, and his rental properties provided little income. Rob would need a healthy environment with someone to help care for him.

Tension brewed as Rob's family discussed where he should live. Some thought he should move back home. Rob didn't want to do that. His mother was a caring woman, but she was also a chain smoker and had some physical limitations. Ultimately, the family agreed Rob would spend the first few days post-hospital at his brother's home.

The surgery went smoothly. Rob even remarked that if all he had to do to keep his tumor away was to have surgery every few years, he would be fine with that. I thought it was strange, but I was happy he was optimistic. He was content to believe that he would beat the odds. Why shouldn't he? He didn't fit the statistical profile. He would go through the treatments and all would be fine.

Even though I had backed out of the work conference and didn't really know where I stood, I spoke with my employer about a more flexible work schedule that would allow me to spend more time with Rob. Thankfully, they agreed to let me work part of each week from home. Other than an occasional required meeting, my job did not depend on a set physical location. It would take some adjusting, though, to make certain I always had the materials with me that I needed to do my job.

Although we had failed at living together before, there was no question in my mind that Rob should move into my house. It was the best option. With my new work schedule, I would be available to care for him. Rob agreed, but he was hesitant to cause a stir with his family. He finally spoke up, left his brother's home, and moved into my house.

Not long after moving in, Rob began the next phase of his treatment, radiation. This involved a long commute to and from a Boston hospital several days each week for many weeks. Rob's family and friends pulled together on this and took turns driving and spending time with him on the days I worked in Boston.

When I worked from home, I took him to his treatments. The clinic featured a calm waiting room with

Treatment Begins

a large fish tank. This room would prove to be very different from the waiting rooms to come. There was also a remarkable parking attendant. It may seem odd to remember a parking attendant, but this man was so full of energy and goodness. He would remember Rob's name and go out of his way to speak a kind word to him. It was like he knew Rob was suffering from a dreadful diagnosis and was determined to ease the burden. He was a drop of sunshine in the middle of a storm.

Aside from a few side effects from the radiation, Rob handled that part of his treatment well. He bounced back quickly between visits and kept himself busy with odd jobs around the house. One day he surprised me. As I returned home from work and opened the door, a large, furry dog with a curled tail stared up at me. Stunned and confused, I entered with caution. Rob and I had talked about getting a dog, had researched breeds, and had even completed some online quizzes to determine which breed was supposedly right for us. But we had not decided on anything.

Well, this dog was not one of the recommended breeds. My slight disappointment at not having been part of choosing the dog with Rob quickly passed as I spent time with her. She was a good-natured mutt that seemed happy to be with us. Rob had adopted her from a shelter. He told me she was about a year and a half old, which I would find out years later was not true. She was closer to six months old. I don't know if he didn't listen to what he was told about her age or if he deliberately told me the wrong thing since we had agreed not to get a puppy. It doesn't really matter. We named her Mandy, which meant worthy to be loved, and she lived up to that name.

CHAPTER 7

California Dreaming

Enjoying cool drinks and a delightful meal while seated at a quaint table outside on a beautiful sunny day in California, we could have been an image on a postcard. I don't remember the name of the restaurant, nor do I remember what we ate, but I remember how pleasant it was to sit there and pretend that all was right with the world. We had come to California in search of answers and in search of hope.

Ever since Rob was first diagnosed, I'd been researching his illness. I wanted to know about the latest treatments and options. What were the causes and contributing factors? Could these be reversed? Did lifestyle and diet matter?

I learned about an upcoming brain tumor convention in California that looked promising for finding answers to my questions. We somehow scraped together enough money to go. Living on only my salary and the rent from Rob's rental properties, with multiple loans and bills to pay each month, our budget was tight. Being a bargain hunter, I scored a cheap hotel through an online bidding site and found the least expensive airfare and car rental possible.

After flying across the country, we were excited to get to the conference. Experts such as physicians, neurosurgeons, oncologists, neuro-oncologists, nutritionists, and representatives from various drug companies were there to present recent research about brain tumors and the latest treatments. It was no paltry affair, and it was impressive.

At first I found it amazing to be in a place surrounded by families in the same situation as us. They were either caring for someone with a brain tumor or suffering from a brain tumor themselves. I couldn't believe so many people were there. My excitement gradually faded into empathy when I realized that those people, like us, were there desperately seeking hope, some alternative medicine or promising procedure, anything that would take the illness away. As we walked around, I could see it in their faces. They all had that look of longing and weariness. I wondered if I had that look too.

One of the bright notes of the conference was when we met a nutritionist. This wasn't just any nutritionist. She was someone who specialized in using nutrition to beat brain cancer. Someone close to her had been diagnosed with a brain tumor, and she devoted her practice to fighting tumor growth. Until this time, we had not thought too much about nutrition. We were young and foolish, eating whatever we wanted. Neither of us was overweight, so we didn't pay attention to what we ate or drank. We had so much to learn. It was this nutritionist who set us on a different path.

After the multi-day conference, we set out to explore California before meeting up with some friends in the area. Although the conference was excellent and we had learned a great deal, it was so nice to just relax, daydream in our picturesque setting, and forget about cancer. It was lovely to get a small glimpse of life in California. I even put my toes in the Pacific Ocean for the first time.

Returning to reality was challenging, but we were refreshed with a new sense of purpose. We would beat this cancer. We had learned many others out there were fighting the same fight and that new treatment options were on the horizon. We felt less powerless and more determined than ever before.

We contacted the nutritionist we had met at the conference, and she recommended a plan. Rob would change his diet and begin taking nutritional supplements. This meant more learning for me since I was the one preparing our meals. I went along with the proposed eating plan partly to support him and partly because after reading the research, I became convinced that it was the path to staying healthy myself. I felt more empowered with this plan. No doom and gloom would fill our home. Rob was young, fit, and had no other health conditions. He didn't fit the tumor profile, and he wasn't a statistic. He was the man that I loved, and we would beat this cancer and live a long healthy life together.

CHAPTER 8

Killing Cancer

The chemotherapy waiting room felt much too small for the number of occupants it held. It was a stark contrast to the tranquil fish-tank environment we had experienced in the radiation waiting area. There was nothing pleasant about this room, and the forlorn faces of the people present made it obvious that absolutely no one wanted to be there. We all just sat quietly in the same dazed stupor.

No one paid much attention when an older woman with a scarf tied around her head attempted to maneuver between the rows of people. I noticed that she did not appear steady on her feet. No sooner did I observe this, when she collapsed. At once, everyone seemed to wake up, as if a bright light had unexpectedly been turned on in a dark room. What had just happened? The hospital staff came to her aid, and within minutes they rolled her away in a wheelchair. I wondered if she would still get her chemotherapy that day. I wondered how many treatments she'd had and if it was even helping.

Killing cancer without further injuring the patient is no minor feat. As I understood it, chemotherapy was supposedly poisonous to cancerous cells. The goal was to kill cancer cells without harming healthy cells.

Making it through the waiting room was step one of an exhausting treatment day. Well, perhaps step one was driving for an hour or more in Boston traffic to get to the hospital. Plus, there was the blood test that you had to get before you even advanced to the chemotherapy waiting room. You had to be healthy enough to receive your poison.

The next challenging part, at least for Rob, came when they finally called his name and led him through the room full of patients all attached to intravenous drips. Once he was sitting in a chair, a nurse would attach his IV. Rob was not a fan of needles. Sometimes this went well, and sometimes it didn't. Then, we would sit there for hours on end watching the level of the IV drip lower. When it was empty, we could go home.

Rob hated chemotherapy. I hated what chemotherapy did to him. As if the infusions themselves were not bad enough, there were side effects. Rob would get weak and sick to his stomach. He often felt too ill to leave the house. Normally an active guy who liked to work and play, the effects made him miserable. Despite his suffering, he was brave and determined to get through it. I would take him to his sessions and other appointments on the days I worked from home, and family or friends would take him on the other days.

Even though we were optimistic at the start of his treatment, that optimism faded a little with each MRI scan. The chemotherapy was not working as the doctor had hoped. I can't remember how many sessions Rob finished before the medication was first changed, or how many more times the doctor changed it. Each time Rob tried a new chemotherapy, it felt like we were playing the lottery and hoping for the jackpot.

While it was difficult to predict what Rob could eat and how often, I tried to follow the plan his nutritionist recommended. She was familiar with the different medications he took, and she made suggestions based on his symptoms. When Rob began losing weight, a scary side effect for someone who is already thin, the focus changed to getting as many calories as possible into him. Nutritional drinks became a staple of his diet.

With so much to tend to at home, there was little time for anything else. Many of my days consisted of an early morning train into Boston and then cramming as much work as possible into the day so I would have less work to bring home. I spent lunch hours, when I took them, shopping for things that Rob and I needed so I wouldn't have to spend time away from him when home. This was tricky, though, because few stores near my office had what I needed or at a price I could afford. Supporting the two of us on just my income challenged me.

Rob's financial situation slightly improved when he decided to "sell" his life insurance. Maybe I should have advised him against that, but it was his decision to make. He had two mortgages and a second mortgage, and the rentals had become a loss. My salary barely covered our basic living expenses. I had a mortgage, car payment, and college loans to pay each month.

In a magazine we saw an advertisement for a company that purchased life insurance policies from people with life-threatening diseases. Technically, the company would become the beneficiary of the policy. They based the amount they would pay for the policy on the prognosis of the applicant. Rob's prognosis was poor, so the payment offer he received was close to the full value of the insurance policy. Rob saw this as a positive thing. He was still so determined to beat the odds that he even joked about the company making a bad financial decision. This payment, along with some unexpected funds that he received later, eased the financial burden in our household, and we focused on getting Rob healthy.

CHAPTER 9

Back to Counseling

Walking into the counseling center that evening was like every other time before. There was no one at the front desk behind the unfriendly wall of glass that separated the "well" from the "unwell" to check me in, as usual, so I sat in the empty seating area and waited. This was my night to see the psychiatrist. As always, I didn't want to be there. I was tired from working all day, and the fact that I had to be there at all troubled me. The psychiatrist was usually unpleasant and often seemed like he didn't want to be there either.

Weeks earlier, during a routine medical visit, my primary care doctor asked how I was doing emotionally. My doctor knew that I had been treated for depression in the past. When I'd mentioned Rob's diagnosis and prognosis, she became concerned for both of us. She suggested I seek counseling, and I agreed to go. Given that I needed to be at my best to help Rob and I was struggling to keep up with everything, it seemed wise. Maybe this time would be better. I just needed to find the right person.

Thankfully, I found a local therapist that I liked. She

was a kind woman that would leave a lasting impact. Even so, I fell into the trap of accepting my previous diagnosis of depression as a permanent characteristic. Looking back, I'm not sure I was clinically depressed—more like just tired and overwhelmed by my responsibilities and Rob's diagnosis. However, when you've assumed for a long time that you are defective, it is difficult to see yourself any other way. You answer the psychological profile questions in such a way as to guarantee the diagnosis you have already predetermined in your mind. I believed that I suffered from depression and behaved accordingly. Even though I probably just needed someone to offer support and practical advice, I became convinced, again, that I was broken and that medication would fix me.

It is sad that once you've gone down the medication road, future therapists and physicians seem all too eager to go down that same road. It doesn't matter whether the road was the right one to take in the first place.

My therapist was not licensed to prescribe medication, so taking medication required regular visits to the counseling center's psychiatrist. This psychiatrist was not like my counselor. He was cold.

After quite some time waiting for the psychiatrist to call my name, another patient came in, stopped at the desk, and sat down. By this time, a receptionist was at the front desk. I considered going up to the desk, but I didn't move. Surely the receptionist noticed I was sitting there waiting. More time went by. I should have said something, but I wasn't one to question things back then. I just waited and kept to myself.

Besides, I was used to waiting for doctors. It was nothing new. Sometimes Rob and I had to wait an hour or

Back to Counseling

more to see his neuro-oncologist. At the counseling center, the front desk was almost always vacant when I arrived for my visits. I didn't know if the center was understaffed or if the receptionist just preferred to not sit at her post, but at some point, she would always appear at her desk before the doctor walked out to call my name.

More time passed. Then instead of looking in the waiting area to see if I was there, from the hallway, the doctor called the other patient's name. Now I became concerned. I had been sitting there for a long time, and the other patient had come in a long time after I arrived.

With anger brewing inside of me like a hot steaming kettle about to whistle, I mustered the courage to go up to the receptionist and ask why I had not been called. With no heartfelt apologies, her response was, "You didn't check-in." Check-in? No one was at the desk to check-in. No one is ever at the desk to check-in! Was that my fault? Evidently, yes.

When I had first noticed that the receptionist had returned to her post, I suppose I should have checked in. However, I had not checked in countless times before. No one ever suggested that I should have checked in on all the other nights when the desk had been vacant at my arrival. She must have known I was expected, since I had an appointment. I was not invisible. If she had bothered to look over at the waiting area, she would have seen me there. I was furious.

Now, someone else may have just left at this point, since now I had to wait until the other patient finished his appointment before I could be seen, if I could be seen at all. Someone else might have just made another appointment and come back another day instead of wasting any more time. But I couldn't do that. I had to be seen on this day because my prescription needed to be refilled, and this doctor was in control of refilling it. If I didn't get a refill, then I would go without my antidepressant, and if I went without the antidepressant, then I would go through withdrawal. I did not want to go through that. I had been through withdrawal before when doctors would experiment with different medications and dosages. It was awful. There was no time for sickness from medication changes when I had Rob to care for at home. I felt helpless. The system had me in its clutches, and I could do nothing about it. I was trapped.

So I waited, again. After the doctor finally finished with the other patient, the receptionist sent me in. I remember not even looking at him. I was so upset. He attempted to voice a weak, insincere apology for the confusion but then squarely placed the blame on me. I lashed out with my questions as tears filled my eyes, surprising myself that I let my emotions surface so vividly in front of a stranger. He offered no answers for why no one bothered to look in the waiting area to see if I was there, even though I had never missed an appointment and was always on time.

Empty and exhausted, I shut down after this and had no more words for him. I got my prescription and left, defeated by the system that was supposed to be helping me.

CHAPTER 10

A Lonely Wedding Day

The sun shone brightly on that warm summer day in the Bahamas. Most everyone else on the cruise ship had gone ashore for an adventure or for relaxation, but not us. This was our wedding day, and the ceremony would begin soon. I stood in front of a tiny mirror in our little cabin, frantically fixing my hair. Rob had already left to go to the room that would serve as our wedding sanctuary.

As a special treat, I had booked an appointment to have my hair styled. This may not seem unusual for a bride on her wedding day, but it was for me. I didn't splurge on things like that, and I wasn't a girl who sought pampering. However, I thought it would be nice to hire a professional to make my hair look special for our wedding day.

At the salon, there was a communication gap with my stylist, and I left disappointed. Part of that disappointment was with myself because I didn't speak up when I had the chance. I had requested long, loose curls. Although her command of the English language was not perfect, the stylist seemed to understand what I wanted. She washed, dried, and then set my hair in curlers. When the stylist removed the curlers, I was optimistic. There was just the right amount of curl. A little finessing and some hairspray, and it would have been perfect.

Then it was ruined. After playing with my hair a little, the stylist grabbed a brush and pulled it through my locks, thus removing my curls and leaving a frizzy poufy mess. I should have stopped her. Why didn't I stop her? Instead, I just assumed that she knew what she was doing. Trying hard to control my emotions, I paid for the service and left as quickly as I could.

When I returned from the salon, Rob was so sweet. He didn't judge or show any reaction to my hairstyle. He just gently said "Do you like it?" I think he knew by the look on my face I didn't. I wanted to cry, but I had already done my makeup. Crying would have ruined it, and there was no time to redo it. I needed what little time I had left to fix my hair and dress for our wedding. Rob had gotten ready while I was at the salon. He looked so handsome in his suit and hat. He had lost his hair from the cancer treatments and had purchased a nice hat to wear for the wedding.

Since there wasn't much time until the ceremony was scheduled to begin, Rob went to stall the folks involved—a local minister, a coordinator, and a photographer. The coordinator had escorted us earlier to get our official marriage documents on the island where the ship docked. It all seemed odd, but also exciting.

As soon as Rob left the cabin, I tried to calm myself down. As I looked in the mirror, it suddenly dawned on me that I was getting ready for my wedding alone. It felt wrong, so wrong. Where were my bridesmaids? I had none. Where was my maid-of-honor? I didn't have one.

Where were my mom and sister and the rest of my family? They were home. We had done this alone, all alone. Rob didn't want a big wedding, and we had agreed that it would probably be too emotional for our families and friends, given his condition. We had convinced ourselves that a low-key wedding would be best. At that moment, getting ready for our wedding all alone in that cabin, I regretted our decision.

The decision to get married came not long before the cruise. Rob and I had discussed getting married many times in the past, but within a brief time of living together, his illness and the uncertainty of the future brought marriage center stage. It felt like the time was right. We would get married and meet the challenge of keeping him healthy together.

Even though I had long since disposed of my fairy-tale wedding planning binder, part of me still longed for that dream wedding. I was sad to let that go, but my priorities had shifted. We had to do what we thought was right for everyone. Besides, by this time I knew that Rob was not a prince. He was simply the man that I loved and the man who loved me. That was all that mattered, and I would stand by him no matter what.

Though neither of us had cruised before, getting married while on a cruise to the Bahamas sounded like a good option. The cruise company offered wedding packages and handled all the details. Plus, it came with a modest price tag we could afford.

The time leading up to the wedding resembled traditional wedding planning. My mom and I went dress shopping. I had a bridal shower. We even planned a reception at a local hall. We made favors and table decorations. We hired a disc jockey, and our family members volunteered to make food and bring supplies. The only differences were that the reception would take place after we returned from the cruise and no one would actually attend the wedding.

We had timed the wedding so it would happen when Rob was feeling his best between chemotherapy treatments. His condition had slightly improved, and we were blindly optimistic. His treatment at this time consisted of daily oral chemotherapy medication for one week every month. That meant he felt poorly during the week of treatment and usually the week after. This was usually followed by two weeks of feeling relatively well.

The oral medication regimen was a welcome change to IV chemotherapy. There were no more lengthy, tiring trips into the city for treatment with needles and crowded waiting rooms. His medication was delivered to our home each month. There were still appointments to have blood levels checked, but those were done locally, and the results were sent electronically to his neuro-oncologist.

We were both hopeful this medicine would work. The drug had been part of a clinical trial in its last stage when Rob began using it, but was later approved as a treatment option. This medication regimen made it possible for us to go away for our wedding.

Trying to keep my emotions under control, I took some deep breaths as I gazed into the mirror. It suddenly occurred to me that I could order room service. Surely some wine would help me relax and forget about being alone on my wedding day. Thankfully, the knock on my door came quickly. I sipped at the wine as I worked on my hair. As soon as I was satisfied I had given it my best effort,

A Lonely Wedding Day

I put on my fancy dress and shoes and off I went.

I don't know how long it took me to get ready and walk the long hallway to the elevator and then find the ceremony location on the ship, but I do remember the smile on Rob's face when I saw him. He was beaming! Relieved to see him happy, and at ease with his company, I let go of the guilt brewing inside of me for having delayed our wedding.

The ceremony felt like it was over before it even started. We went to another room for our wedding cake and some champagne. Then it was off to the deck for some photos. Before we knew it, we were back in our cabin. Wedding over. I don't know if it was the stress of the morning or the champagne and the wine that I drank, but I was extremely tired. Rob called home to tell his mom we were officially married, and I took a nap.

With the wedding behind us, it was easier to relax during the rest of the cruise. One day we went parasailing. Another day we lounged on a beach and swam in the beautifully clear water.

Besides our island fun, we also enjoyed activities on the ship. The day after our wedding, we took part in a game show in one of the large theater-type rooms. It was like the "Newlywed Game," and the host chose couples from the audience. When he asked for a couple who had been married the shortest time, I raised my hand tall since we had been married less than a day. I think Rob was both surprised and embarrassed. It was not in my nature to volunteer to go up on a stage in front of a sizeable group of people, but I knew it was a once-in-a-lifetime opportunity, and I was not passing it up. Besides, we were now officially on our honeymoon, and we needed to celebrate. The host invited us to be contestants, and we joined a few other couples on the stage.

In this fun game, the couples had their backs to each other and wrote answers to various questions. The goal was to match the responses of their spouse. The host interjected with quirky commentary to amuse the audience. We got most of the questions right, but the couple who had been married the longest performed better. The audience found it especially funny when the question was "What did you do after your wedding?" and our answers were "took a nap." Afterward, Rob was glad we took part in the game. We enjoyed the rest of the cruise and tried our best to forget about cancer.

CHAPTER 11

Saved by Grace

Sitting in my counselor's office, I didn't know that my life was about to change and my husband's along with it. I don't recall what we talked about or whether the counseling was even helping, but I remember what she said to me that day. She strongly recommended that Rob and I find a church to attend.

When I look back now, it was rather risky for her to suggest such a thing since she worked for a secular counseling center. It was an unusual recommendation, and I didn't understand why she thought it would help. Now that I think about it, I am awestruck at the blessing this counselor bestowed by her suggestion.

So I considered her recommendation and discussed it with Rob later that day. If my counselor thought it would somehow help us stay strong while battling cancer, maybe it was worth a try. Anything was worth a try.

For several years during my early childhood, I'd attended a church and was baptized there. So if someone had asked me, I would have said that I was protestant, because that was the denomination of the church I'd attended. I assumed that meant I was a Christian. I was not. I believed in the existence of God, but I grew up without faith. My only knowledge of religion was what I had learned in some required classes at the Catholic college I'd attended. Even though the college prided itself on accepting students of various faiths, some religious classes were mandatory.

Rob had been actively involved in a church as a child, but he'd strayed from it as a teen. Although we both thought we believed in God, neither of us behaved as a Christian or even really knew what it meant to be one. Sure, we felt that we were "good people" and tried to do what we thought was right, but we lived for ourselves. That is not to say that we didn't help others. We did. However, our lives held no deeper meaning or purpose. The focus was on us, and most recently, the focus was on Rob's health. Somewhere inside, we both longed for more. We decided to give church a try.

Attending a church would be a big change for us. It had to be convenient. Giving up Sunday was a lot to ask. I shudder to think about our attitudes back then. Being my typical research-driven self, I got to work looking for the right church to suit our needs. It had to be relatively close to where we lived, with convenient service times, preferably not late weekend mornings. It just so happened that the church Rob attended as a child held informal Thursday evening services. Perfect. We didn't have to give up our Sundays.

I can still remember walking into the church those first few times. Everyone was so welcoming and appeared genuinely excited to have us there. This behavior was new to me, and I was distrustful. Who were these people, and why were they being so friendly and kind? There was just something different about them. I didn't know then it was the Lord.

I can still picture the pastor and the assistant pastor with their hands held out, eager to shake our hands and welcome us each week. There were many others too. There was an elderly couple who seemed to pour out joy, and others who always made a point to speak with us. I was continually amazed at their kindness. The short sermons were insightful and encouraging, and the singing of hymns was fun. But it was the love that these folks showed us that kept us coming back week after week.

Rob especially seemed to enjoy the chitchat before and after the evening service. Although he could be shy in certain circumstances, he was a people person at heart and thrived on being with others. For whatever reason, before we attended that first church service, Rob had decided to keep his diagnosis quiet. He didn't want the folks at church to know he was fighting cancer. Maybe he thought people would treat him differently if they knew. I went along with his decision since it was not my tale to tell, but eventually he found the right moment to share it.

As time went on, someone suggested to Rob that we might like to attend the Sunday morning service. This would be a gigantic step for us. The Sunday morning service was "real church." We weren't sure if we were ready for that. We enjoyed the informality of the evening services with the small gathering of the same people each week and the casual attire. They held Sunday services in the large sanctuary. I feared the number of people, the formality, and the time commitment. Would we still enjoy going to church?

Thankfully, we tried it. It was different, but not in a

bad way, and Sunday morning church gradually became part of our weekly routine. The pastor preached with such passion that we left each service full of inspiration for the week ahead. We looked forward to going to church each week.

It was at one of the Sunday morning services that I accepted Jesus into my heart. Ever since that first evening church service, something had been stirring inside of me. I wanted to know the love that the folks there poured out. I wanted to understand the mystery of their faith. They did not practice a religion. Their belief affected every cell of their being. It was clear in their expressions, behavior, and speech. How could that be? It boggled my mind and opened my eyes to the shallowness and emptiness I felt inside. I wanted to know the Lord as they did.

Even with all that I had gone through with caring for Rob, I was not living with a sense of a greater purpose. How could I? I thought I was defective. I was a shy, quiet girl with anxiety and depression, caring for a sick husband. I was damaged. The more I attended church, the more I learned that the Bible is full of damaged people who did magnificent things. The pastor would often tell stories of present-day heroes in the faith. They all were broken at some point, but they rose above their circumstances to serve others.

Every so often at the end of his sermons, the pastor would say a special prayer, a prayer of salvation. He would invite anyone willing to accept Jesus to recite the prayer silently to themselves. One Sunday morning, I decided to pray that special prayer. My life changed that day, and interestingly, Rob's did, too. He told me after the service that he had also prayed the prayer. We had both made a decision for Christ at the same time. How amazing is that?

So now we were both new Christians. I felt a refreshing sense of peace and purpose. I had put my trust in something outside of myself. I was learning to acknowledge that God was in control and that there was a reason for my existence in the world. Even if I was damaged, I could still be useful.

Not long after our decision for Christ, the assistant pastor, who was a few years younger than us, started a Bible study for young couples and invited us to join. We met regularly with other believers for fellowship and study. It was an exciting time for us, like a new beginning. The more I learned, the more I wanted to learn. Scripture was a mystery that would unveil itself in little pieces. I took it in as it came and tried to apply it to my life.

Rob and I grew even closer as we began to put our selfish ways behind us. Rob's health continued to improve, and we were optimistic about the future. Our new faith compounded this optimism. Surely, now that we knew the Lord and were growing in our faith, He would reward us. It took us a long time to realize that it didn't work that way. All we knew then was that life was looking up.

CHAPTER 12

Answered Prayer

Lying on a hard table in the most awkward of positions, I waited for the long needle. Rob stood by my side, as he had done twice before. I was anxious and tense. This was our last shot, literally and figuratively. I longed for a child, a special blessing that Rob and I could experience together. This was our chance.

Months of specialized medications, lifestyle changes, diet restrictions, and regular visits to a fertility clinic located miles away had taken its toll on me. I wasn't certain if the procedure would work, and neither was my doctor. If it didn't, the next step would involve a surgical test, and that would mean taking time off work. That was not an option. I was still telecommuting from home a few days each week to be with Rob; I couldn't ask for time off.

Although my employer had been generous with my schedule, other coworkers and my supervisors had grown weary of my absences. Working from home was not the norm, and they didn't like it. I sensed their disapproval when I was in the office, and I was uncertain if my job was in jeopardy.

The decision to pursue intrauterine insemination

(IUI) was a long time in the making. Rob's MRI scans seemed to show that the oral chemotherapy regimen was keeping the tumor away. However, the medication in his system could pass through his bodily fluids. That meant that even if he was not sterile from the radiation and chemotherapy, it was not safe to conceive naturally.

Having children was something Rob and I had discussed long before his illness in the early years of our courtship. We both wanted kids and looked forward to the possibility of being parents someday. When Rob became sick and was told that sterility could be a side effect of cancer treatment, he took the necessary steps to preserve his sperm. Even so, his illness weighed heavily on his mind, and the possibility of fathering a child was scary to him. We spent many months discussing it.

Even though we were optimistic about his prognosis and were determined that he would get well, I felt like we shouldn't wait to start a family. We had already waited so long to get married, and my biological clock was ticking away. Plus, part of me feared the future. What would happen if he got sick again? I didn't want to wait to find out. Ultimately, we agreed that we would do some traveling and then pursue pregnancy.

To say that we were naïve travelers when we ventured to Italy would be a gross understatement. Although I read many travel guides and spent hours rehearsing common phrases, I was not prepared for our trip. Rob was even less so, and he trusted that I would guide him. But what did I know about traveling in a foreign country? The only place outside of the United States that I had ever traveled to was Canada, and that was as a child with my family. The only thing that I knew about travel in Italy was what I read about and what a friend of mine had told me about her trip. Basically, we were clueless.

Our once-in-a-lifetime trip to Italy came with many obstacles. We had difficulty finding food in off hours when we strayed from the touristy areas. We both caught a viral infection and experienced what it was like to search for over-the-counter cold medicine in a drugstore where you can't read the labels.

We also had difficulty with transportation. Thinking we could just hop a train or plane to travel to unfamiliar places in the country whenever we wanted, we kept our plans loose by only booking the first few nights of our trip. This was a mistake that we immediately regretted when we boarded an overpacked train and stood like sardines for hours. Fortunately, we learned our lesson and enlisted help from a local travel agency for our remaining train travel.

Even though we faced many difficulties, it was an amazing adventure. We strolled the Italian streets. The beauty of the architecture and the depth of the history overwhelmed us. We enjoyed some fabulous meals, and I gained a new appreciation for coffee. However, by the time our trip neared its end, we were tired and ready to go home.

A few months after we returned home from Italy, I began treatment at the fertility center. My case was different from other infertility cases in that it was unknown whether I could get pregnant without intervention. So the doctor used medications and monitoring to improve my chances of a successful pregnancy. The medications came with some side effects. As my hormone levels changed, my mood changed with them.

During the time of the infertility treatment, Rob and I traveled to a brain tumor conference in Florida with Rob's sister and her husband. Even though things were looking up, we were still trying to stay educated about the latest research and options. It was nice to have Rob's family with us, but I felt cranky and unwell. Since we were keeping the fertility treatment a secret, I couldn't explain the reason for my extreme moodiness. I can't recall whether we learned about any new treatments at the conference, but just attending made us feel more empowered.

Back in Massachusetts, I anxiously waited for the needle. Although I had been through the IUI process twice before, this time would be different. The technician came in to speak with us moments before the procedure. She asked a simple yet powerful question no one had asked before: "Would you like to say a prayer before we begin?"

I'm sure I had prayed silently before the other procedures, but never aloud with my husband in front of someone else. It seemed strange to be asked the question, but I also felt an enormous peace. It was as if the Lord was commanding us to take a deep breath, calm down, stay in the moment, and focus on the fact that He was in control.

I don't know why the question was asked. Maybe I was wearing my cross necklace that day. Maybe I had to fill out a religious affiliation on a registration form. My faith tells me that the Lord used that woman to speak to us that day. I am thankful that He did. We needed to put our focus on prayer. We needed the reminder that our faith came first. No matter what the future held, it was out of our hands. Maybe we would have a child. Maybe we wouldn't. It wasn't up to us. It was up to God. Our faith needed to be strong for the days ahead. Thankfully, the Lord answered our prayer that day.

Nine months later we had a son.

CHAPTER 13

Becoming a Mother

With a red pen in hand, a stack of manuscript pages on the table in front of me, and my baby boy nursing himself to sleep on my chest, I got to work. After our son, Noah, was born, I did not return to my editing job. I had hoped to work full time from home, but my employer was not willing to offer me that option. They did, however, offer to provide me with occasional freelance work if I left. So I left my job and became a self-employed stay-at-home mom, completing assignments for my former employer and other educational publishing companies.

Even though most nights did not involve sound sleep, Noah took regular naps during the day. This gave me enough time to get my work done. Sure, I probably should have used that time to nap myself, but I chose not to. I was so happy to be home full time, and I was determined to make it work. Rob, on the other hand, was not so sure. He had grown accustomed to me working full time, and I think it made him nervous that I had left the security of my job.

Financially we were fine. We had paid off our debts, lived beneath our means, and the rental properties plus my freelance assignments provided enough income to sustain us. Since Rob's scans had been clear several times and he was feeling stronger, he began to build his HVAC business again. Many days he wasn't even home.

Oh, those early days of motherhood were as magical as they were tiring and nerve-racking. Learning to be responsible for an infant was no small feat, and I struggled at first, trying so hard to do everything "right." Breastfeeding was challenging at first. My milk arrived with such force that I could not nurse our son. I can't recall how the arrangements were made with our lactation consultant, but I remember that Rob went to meet someone and brought back an electric breast pump. He was my superhero. The pump helped enormously, and breastfeeding got easier.

Having learned so much about cancer and potential causes, I was extremely cautious with Noah. I used natural products for bathing, skin care, and laundry. We even used cloth diapers instead of disposable. That required extra work, but I felt like it was worth it. I tried to eat healthy so as to pass on beneficial nutrients through my breast milk. Caffeine had been mostly eliminated during pregnancy, and I continued to be careful with my consumption.

I put a lot of pressure on myself, but first-time moms often do. Once I established a daily routine and learned to trust my instincts, I became more confident. I filled my days with nursing, walks with Noah in a stroller, one-on-one playtime, and editing during his naps.

Some days when I didn't have freelance work, I would take our son shopping. I loved showing him new places, and he looked at the unfamiliar sites with much interest. It was wonderful to be out wandering around a store in the middle of the day. I was used to cramming my shopping in during evenings and weekends. Shopping at a leisurely pace during the day, with few crowds and a flexible schedule, gave me a fresh sense of freedom and an appreciation for an existence outside of the typical nine-to-five workday. I felt so fortunate to have left the rat race behind and knew I didn't want to return to it.

Although Rob kept busy during much of the week with his business, on the weekends we enjoyed local family outings. We visited parks, beaches, and nature trails. Sometimes we even brought Mandy along. She had adjusted quickly to having a baby in the house, and her good nature made her an excellent companion on our little adventures.

One weekend during Noah's first year, we drove to Mystic, Connecticut. Though we were only there a few days, I guess you could say it was our first family vacation. Noah loved seeing the exhibits at Mystic Aquarium. I let myself look forward to a future with many such outings.

The days passed so quickly when Noah was little, and it seemed like he learned something new every day. I loved watching him learn. The older he got, the more fun playtime became, with music, interactive toys, and engaging books. It was an unknown world, and I embraced it completely much of the time.

As much as I enjoyed being a new mother, sometimes I struggled. Noah never slept well at night and woke up repeatedly. Those were tough nighttime moments, as he would scream and my level of anxiety would spike. Rob would often defer to me to calm the baby, like I knew what I was doing or like it was my job. This made me even more frustrated.

Looking back, he probably deferred to me since calming our son sometimes involved nursing him back to sleep. When that wasn't the case and the screaming continued, I would sing. I can still remember singing the chorus from the hymn "Sanctuary" over and over again. It was not just to soothe Noah. I was also singing it to myself. In those moments of extreme tiredness, frustration, and stress, I needed a reminder of the woman I wanted to be. Singing that song again and again forced me to calm down, forget my own needs, and focus on the most important need at hand, which was getting my helpless child back to sleep.

CHAPTER 14

Building a Distraction

Staring at the large group of pens on the table, all identical in their style with the attorney's name on the side, I felt uneasy. What were we doing? Should we be spending a sizeable chunk of our savings on a real estate investment? What if it didn't work out?

It's funny how easily you can distract yourself from reality when it seems like everything is going well. We were finally in a time of rest. Why didn't we just stay there and enjoy it? Since Rob's scans had continued to be consistently clear, his doctor suggested that Rob stop chemotherapy. I'm uncertain if Rob thought he was cured, but we were both thankful and thrilled that his cancer appeared to be gone.

Rob was finally back to his usual self, full of energy and drive. I was enjoying being a stay-at-home mom and completing freelance work as it came. Life was good—at least better than it had been in a long time. We were still living in my small one-bedroom house, but Rob had made many improvements and it suited us well, except for the location. Although it was a delightful town and we had lovely neighbors that Rob had all befriended, the noise from the highway that ran behind our home and the planes flying back and forth to the nearby airport left us longing for a quieter place to live.

Over the years, we had spent time in western Massachusetts, New Hampshire, and Vermont and were drawn to their peacefulness and vast open spaces. We would always pick up the local real estate magazines when there and discuss relocating.

In reality, we didn't want to move too far away from our family and friends—we just wanted some quiet open space of our own. Maybe it was because Rob was finally feeling better or maybe it just seemed like the right time, but the desire to move turned into a more frequent and serious discussion, which turned into a decision to look for property in nearby towns.

Rob had always wanted to build his own house. Even though we both loved antique homes with their unique styles and architectural features, Rob knew from experience that they could be a challenge to maintain. He had the construction knowledge to build a new house to his specifications and wanted to put that knowledge to use.

We drove around and looked at houses, discussing the architectural details that we admired. We talked about rooms and floors and windows. He then spent hours drawing building plans and constructing a three-dimensional scaled cardboard model of our future home. All we had to do was find some suitable land to build it. This proved more difficult than we'd thought it would be. Everything within our set price range had serious issues. Some had power lines or easements running through the middle of them. Others did not have enough space to build or were in inaccessible locations.

As the months went on, and when we didn't find what we were looking for, we expanded our search. Our new goal became trying to find a house in need of repair on a sizeable piece of land. Rob would restore the house, we would subdivide the property into two lots, sell the renovated house, and build our new home on the vacant lot. It sounded easy enough.

It wasn't long before I found a listing online for a property that sounded promising. I remember the day that we first looked at the property. The existing house was crammed full of stuff, so much so you couldn't see most of the interior. The garage and the vehicles parked on the property were the same way, completely packed. There were school buses full of who knows what. Rob seemed to overlook the hoarding situation and saw potential in the house. I think he was just eager to see the land.

The weather that day was cold, and viewing the rest of the property required walking down a long gravel path to get to it. We didn't care about being out in the cold, because walking the path would lead us to a decision. Was the land suitable for building our dream home or not? Noah was bundled up on my chest in a sling. This was to be a family experience.

To my dismay, the real estate agent insisted it was too cold to bring our son for the walk. She told us a horror story about a child who'd gotten sick from the cold. Maybe it was a sales tactic so she could convince Rob of the property's merits without me present. I don't know, but Rob didn't want to argue with her. He suggested that I wait in the car with Noah instead of seeing the land.

I wish I could have seen Rob's first reaction, because

he was so excited when he finally returned to the car. He thought the property was perfect. It was mostly wooded with a large cornfield that had potential as a building site. He was completely smitten.

So despite the condition of the house, the amount of work it would take to improve it, and the fact that we didn't even know if the land could be subdivided or built on, he wanted to buy the property. It would be a risk, but we decided it was a risk worth taking. He knew what it would take to fix the house, and I trusted him. He insisted it was mostly cosmetic and wouldn't be difficult.

After going back and forth with the sellers, who didn't seem like they were ready to sell—even though the property had been for sale a long time—we finally reached an agreement. Though it wasn't without concessions. We agreed to allow the current owners to stay in the house for a set time period so they could find other housing and remove their belongings, including the vehicles on the property. It was more than a little nerve-racking wondering if the sellers would keep up their end of the agreement. Sitting at the closing, I was worried. Over the years, Rob had rented to some less-than-stellar tenants who were downright awful. I was not eager to take on more tenants, even if it was only for a brief time.

Thankfully, before long, the house was empty, and Rob went full speed ahead in repairing it. He had left cancer behind and was fully focused on this new project. He even purchased a used backhoe and an old tractor to help him work. It would be less expensive to own than rent, was what he told me. It made sense and it made him happy. I couldn't argue with that.

CHAPTER 15

Surprise! You're Not Sterile

My doctor just stared at me in disbelief. Perhaps she thought I was crazy. She knew my history of anxiety and depression. Maybe she thought I had ventured into the land of delusions. "Why do you think you are pregnant?" she asked me.

I understood her disbelief. I was still breastfeeding, and my menstrual cycle had not yet returned. Besides that, my husband was supposedly sterile. After all the cancer treatments he had been through and countless consent forms he had signed that mentioned the sterility side effect, he had to be sterile. I couldn't possibly be pregnant.

I mustered up the courage to speak and told my doctor about my extreme tiredness and unusual cramps. Then I admitted that I had taken an at-home pregnancy test that had come back positive. The fact that I was even at the doctor's office was a testament to my disbelief. I knew something was going on with my body, but I wasn't convinced I was pregnant. For many women, one at-home test may have been enough proof. To me, two tests weren't enough. I needed my doctor to tell me, especially after all that we'd gone through to get pregnant with our first child.

Even though I don't think my doctor was convinced of my perceived condition, she humored me with a pregnancy test. It was positive. Some blood tests followed, and then I was sent home. Now all I had to do was figure out how to tell Rob. He knew what was going on, at least most of it. I'd told him I thought I was pregnant and was going to the doctor to find out. I didn't divulge that I had already taken the two at-home tests.

As soon as I saw him, he wanted to know what the doctor had said, but I didn't want to tell him the news right away. This was such an unexpected miracle, and I wanted the news to come in a memorable way. I told him we needed to wait for the blood test results to be sure, and then I devised a plan.

Even though I was trying to make the announcement special, I felt guilty about keeping it from him. So instead of a complicated plan, I opted for something simple and quick. I purchased some fortune cookies at the grocery store and carefully removed a fortune with a pair of tweezers and then replaced it with another slip of paper. I gave Rob the special cookie when he came home. When he cracked it open and read "Guess what!" on the paper inside, it didn't take any time at all for him to guess correctly. Unbelievably, we were having another baby!

CHAPTER 16

Eat, Vomit, Repeat

Leaving our cozy tiny house that day was hard, really hard. I didn't want to go. Traveling back and forth each day from our home to our new property had become too much for Rob. Sometimes he made multiple trips because he needed tools or supplies. It became apparent, at least to him, that it made sense for us to move into the partially restored house. The house was almost finished, and whatever was left could be accomplished more easily while living there. Then he could concentrate on building our new home on the land. It made sense from his point of view. It would be easier and less stressful for him to be there.

Financially, I wasn't sure it made sense. The original plan had been to stay in our house until our dream home was built. Our little home was worth about half of the other house. Finishing the other house, selling it, and then using that money to fund the new house made more sense to me.

Compounding my desire to stay was the fact that I was still emotionally attached to our home. I had worked hard to purchase it on my own. Besides that, we'd started our married life together in that house, and our family. I had decorated a little area as a nursery and made curtains. Rob had redone the kitchen and built a lovely porch, which I adored.

Sure it was small, but I was perfectly content to stay in that house until our new home was built, even it was an old, tiny one-bedroom house with mice running through the walls. I wasn't ready to leave.

The new house had always seemed like a distant dream, something to look forward to. Now, I was being asked to sell my house, move to another town, and hope that we could build our house. We still didn't even know if we could build on the land. Plus, I was newly pregnant. We had not even told our families yet. Now we would have to tell them because they would help us move and it would be noticeable that I wasn't lifting much, to protect the baby.

Fortunately, the move went smoothly, and I reluctantly adjusted to living in the other house. I refused to unpack everything, though, because it was supposed to be only a temporary living situation. I tucked packed boxes away from sight and looked forward to the day when I would open them in our new home.

I must admit, it was nice to walk down the dirt path to our planned future building site and dream. Noah loved gathering rocks and playing in the dirt as we went. Mandy loved the new property, too. No longer was she bound by a small fenced yard. We finally had our own open, quiet space.

Rob finished restoring the house and worked with an architect to finalize our new house plans. Then came endless meetings with the town. There were issues with getting permission to build.

Over time, Rob had become more involved with our church, volunteering for committees, doing missionary projects, and attending meetings. Between dealing with the architect's constant mistakes, the town politics, maintaining his business, and being present for church responsibilities, the carefree man I loved became stressed as we waited for our baby's arrival. He was doing too much.

More than a week after my due date, the Lord blessed us with another son, Luke. Shortly after delivery, I hemorrhaged, passed out, and frightened Rob. I saw his panicked look when I regained consciousness. A doctor and several nurses surrounded me. The doctor was barking orders to administer some medicine, and someone was pushing on my belly. I didn't know what was going on.

During the ordeal of trying to get my bleeding under control, my tray of food was taken away. When I realized it was gone, I wanted to scream. Instead, I cried. I had not eaten in many hours. My food had just arrived, and I had only managed a few mouthfuls before I'd fainted. It might have seemed silly to be upset about food just after a medical emergency, but I was hungry, hormonal, and had been looking forward to that post-delivery meal.

With Noah not yet two, I had my hands full when I arrived home from the hospital. Caring for a baby and a toddler was challenging. Then there was the breastfeeding. I'm not sure how long it took before we realized that something was wrong. A strange pattern began. Luke would cry because he was hungry. I would nurse him, burp him, nurse him some more, and burp him again. All would be well for a few minutes. He would be perfectly content. Then without warning, he would projectile vomit and let out a blood-curdling cry.

Again and again the cycle repeated. Each feeding was like this. Naps were not much better. If you put him down, he would scream. The only way that he would go to sleep was in someone's arms, in his swing, or in his car seat. He had to be partially upright.

After doing some research, we suspected he had reflux. However, our pediatrician offered little help, and suggested Luke's symptoms were normal. It wasn't until he began losing weight, instead of gaining it, that she agreed something was wrong. He was feeding all the time, but because he was vomiting so much, he wasn't taking enough nutrients or calories in.

He was diagnosed with reflux. Having tried every remedy except medication, that was our next course of action.

Thankfully, the medicine helped, and the vomiting ceased. All was well again in our family, or so we thought. Little did we know that darkness was lurking just ahead. I wish we could have run away right then, stopped the clock, and lingered in that time longer. Life was happy then. Even with the reflux, the stress of a new baby and an energetic toddler, and the pressures Rob was facing, I still wish I could go back to that time. We were a new family embarking on a new life together. It was a precious time full of optimism. Why did it have to change?

CHAPTER 17

Appointment Day

As I sat and anxiously waited for the phone to ring, my stomach was churning. The day had come for Rob's regularly scheduled MRI and follow-up appointment. This was something Rob and I always did together, and it was an all-day affair. However, this time, I didn't go with him.

Although having a family member watch Noah while we went into Boston for the day would have been feasible, the same could not be said of our newborn son. Luke was not easily comforted by others. Bringing him with us to the hospital for the day seemed like a bad idea, at least to Rob. I think he was concerned about germs. Leaving Luke would have meant pumping breastmilk ahead of time and bringing a pump to the hospital. It wasn't like I could just stop breastfeeding for the day. So it was decided that I would stay home with the kids and someone else would go with Rob. He wanted to go alone, but I suggested that someone go with him to keep him company. He asked his mom, and she agreed.

I can't remember how many times I tried to call him, but it was several. He didn't respond. Worry filled me. It was taking too long. He should have been home by now. This wasn't the first time he had ignored my calls. There were plenty of days when he'd chosen not to return my call right away. Those days were different though. In those days he was partying with his buddies. That was ages ago. Besides, he was with his mom, not his friends. Why was it taking so long?

His scans had been clear for such a long time. Surely nothing had changed. Life was good. We had two beautiful boys, and we were working toward building our dream home. We belonged to a loving church family and were growing in our faith. We would raise our family and grow old together. Sure, there had been stress with the architect and dealing with the town. We weren't sleeping much and were still trying to figure out parenting, but we were functioning. We were determined that everything would be all right.

Finally, the call came. All I remember from the conversation is Rob saying something like "It's not good." He refused to give me specifics over the phone and informed me he was at his mom's house with some of his family and didn't know when he'd be home.

What? Just like that, he shut me out. So I was left to wait alone with the kids and worry. I don't recall how long after the phone call that he arrived home, but it seemed like a long time. He didn't even really speak to me when he came in. He just handed me some papers and said he needed to decide on treatment. His tumor was back.

The hours and days following his appointment are now a blur in my mind. Bits and pieces of information from his doctor's visit came out over time, like how the doctor and nurse had verbally expressed how sorry they were. "They just kept apologizing" is what he told me. It sounded as if they'd given him a death sentence right then and there. I should have insisted on being there for his appointment. I was livid when I found out he didn't even have his mom come into the room with him. Why did he do that? That was why she was there! He'd received the news alone. It stung that I had been forced to choose between being a loving mother and a supportive wife. Why hadn't we just brought the baby with us to the hospital that day?

Although Rob had been previously optimistic about his prognosis, seeds of doubt had been planted in his mind months earlier at a prior doctor's visit. An intern helped that day and made some offhand remark about wanting to know Rob's secret. Rob didn't understand what the guy was talking about, so the intern explained that since Rob had lived longer than most people with his diagnosis that he must have had a secret to staying alive. I think the intern's comment hit a nerve with Rob. Until that day, he hadn't wanted to know the odds. He'd been perfectly content in his ignorance of the severity of his condition. He had been convinced that he would beat cancer and that he was supposed to live. Suddenly, he wasn't so sure.

After that visit, he began asking questions. He wanted to know about other patients we'd met at various conferences. Were they still living? I had to confess that most of them were not. I didn't want to tell him the truth. I didn't want him to know. He was beating the odds, and it was a miracle. He didn't need to know the statistics. They were just numbers. Besides, he was not the typical case. He was younger than most and healthier. His profile did not fit the data. I tried to convince him as best I could, but something had triggered in his brain that day. He didn't speak about it, but the underlying worry must have been with him at this appointment. Maybe that was why he went into the room alone.

CHAPTER 18

Google Desperation

Staring at the computer screen late into the night, I read and attempted to understand the medical jargon in each clinical trial description. It had started with a simple Google search for treatment options. My husband's neuro-oncologist had given him two choices, both clinical trials. I can't even remember what they were supposed to do, but they were both early stage trials. That meant that the trials were not even necessarily effective. In my mind, that meant they were last resorts. Either way, he would also need brain surgery, again, to remove the bulk of the tumor. He didn't have time to play with early stage trials. He needed something that would work now. There had to be another trial out there, and I was determined to find it.

We had been down this road before years earlier when he was first diagnosed, and I had done a great deal of research about his condition then. Rob had attempted several clinical trials before finding the drug that helped him. Why he couldn't just use that medication again wasn't entirely clear. His doctor said his cells would probably be resistant to it or something like that. I disagreed since he hadn't been on any chemotherapy medication in a long time, and it seemed worth trying. But what did I know? I wasn't a doctor. We were trusting the doctor to advise us, and he wasn't advising us at all. He had two clinical trials he could offer, and we were supposed to choose one. Or Rob could seek treatment elsewhere.

Rob was relying on me to advise him, but I didn't know how to do that. I was out of the loop on cancer research and brain tumors. There was a time when I read absolutely everything that I could, just in case it might be helpful. I read about research, treatment, nutrition, and causes. I was obsessed with knowing the latest information. But that was then. For the past two years, my hours had been spent raising babies. I read storybooks and books about childcare, not cancer statistics. I did not know what had changed in the fight against brain tumors, if anything. I was naively optimistic that significant progress had been made.

So even though the hour was late and I should have been sleeping, I was sitting at the computer desperately trying to find something that might save my husband. Noah was asleep, and Luke was sleeping in his rocking swing next to me. I can't remember how many times I restarted the timer on that swing. As long as it kept swinging, he would stay asleep and I could keep searching. I just had to keep searching until I found something. There had to be something.

After a while, Rob took notice of the swing and questioned me. How long had Luke been sitting in the swing? Was that really a good idea? Frustrated with his questions, I tried to convince him it wasn't a problem. Here I was searching for a way to help him beat his cancer, and he was questioning my mothering! Once again I was forced to choose between being a good mother and being a good wife. That struggle would continue to surface throughout the next few months as I attempted to meet the needs of everyone at the same time. It was an impossible feat, and continually having to choose which role to fill was excruciating.

In a last-ditch effort to find answers, I stumbled on information about an upcoming brain tumor conference in Florida. Maybe we could go to that and discover a new promising treatment. We had learned so much at conferences in the past. Surely there was something new that Rob could try. But how could we just go to Florida? Bringing the kids to a conference was not a suitable option, and leaving them behind wasn't either. The decision was simple. Rob would go to the conference and I would stay home.

Thankfully, one of Rob's sisters offered to go with him. I can still remember the frantic drive to the airport. We had been at an appointment with a surgeon in Boston to discuss Rob's upcoming brain surgery. We left without scheduling it because the appointment took so long, and Rob needed to get to the airport. Somehow, we made it there just in time for Rob to catch his flight. I drove away hopeful that Rob would find some answers in Florida.

I'm not sure what happened at the conference. Rob didn't seem to learn of any promising new treatments. Even so, he returned somewhat optimistic. It had been good for him to get away with his sister while he was feeling well. It gave his mood a boost as he prepared for his surgery. The night before he was scheduled to go in, he had me take a photo of him with our two boys. I gladly obliged. They all looked so happy. It's a bittersweet memory now, but I love that photo.

Even though I thought we had everything scheduled correctly, the day of the surgery was riddled with unfortunate events. Early in the morning, we arrived at the hospital for Rob's scheduled MRI that he needed before his surgery. After the scan, we were told to go to another area of the hospital to wait for his surgery. That was when things started going wrong.

We found out we had been told the wrong surgery time. Rob was one of the last surgeries of the day, not one of the first. We should not even have been at the hospital yet. He should not have been scheduled to have his MRI so early. He also should not have stopped eating at the time that he was told. Now, not only would he be waiting all day for his surgery, he would be hungry and weak. That's not how you want to go into surgery.

Another complication was childcare. Noah was with a family member, but I had made other plans for Luke. My mom would care for him for a few hours, and then Rob's sisters would pick him up and bring him to me at the hospital while Rob was in surgery. I had my breast pump with me to use for the first few hours. I didn't want to leave Luke all day, but I wanted to be fully present for Rob before his surgery. I figured that I could nurse and care for Luke while Rob was in surgery and recovery. He would never need to know, so it would not cause any stress. I had it all worked out and thought it was a perfect plan. Everyone's needs would be met.

Now that the surgery time was later, my plan was foiled. I called his sisters. Regrettably, I was too late. They had already picked up Luke and were on their way to the hospital. Now, I had to tell Rob. I felt terrible for admitting that I had kept it from him, and even worse that I was adding more turmoil to an already grueling day. Trying to control an uncontrollable situation had failed. Little did I know that the chaos was only just beginning.

CHAPTER 19

A Man Becomes a Child

It felt strange to be sitting at a town committee meeting when our future was in a state of uncertainty, yet there we were. Despite his illness, Rob still wanted to move forward with our home building plan, and our town had not yet approved the project. This was the first time that I had attended a meeting. All the other times, Rob had gone without me. The house was his project, and he wanted to take the lead. It was his dream to build, and he needed to keep that dream alive, if only to keep his mind from worrying about his deteriorating health. It gave him something to focus on, something he could somewhat control. Besides, I knew nothing about building a house, and I was busy taking care of the boys, and the housework, and the cooking, and most everything else.

But by this night, things had changed, and Rob couldn't go to the meeting by himself, even though he thought he could. I don't know if it was all the medications he was taking or if it was the tumor growing in his head, but Rob was often confused, and his behavior had become erratic. Sometimes he acted like a child trapped in a man's body. He would do things that reminded me of our toddler's behavior. If I questioned him about his actions, he would have no logical explanation.

Rob's surgery did not go as well as we had hoped. Part of the tumor could not be removed because of its location in the brain. That meant that his prognosis was even worse than originally predicted. The more tumor that remained, the easier it was for it to grow and grow quickly. At least, that was how I understood it. His only hope was chemotherapy or a miracle. I prayed relentlessly for a miracle as I helplessly watched my husband's condition worsen and his behavior change.

Rob had times when he became fearful of things that didn't exist. He would think someone was lurking in the house or just outside, and I would have to check all over and try to prove he was mistaken. He became paranoid. I purchased dark curtains to cover the windows because anything that caught his eye outside was a cause for panic. Sometimes he would act peculiar or say strange things that made no sense. It was difficult to know what he was thinking or why.

Other times, he was normal. He would act so much like his old self that I would convince myself he was fine and getting better. Then the strange behavior would return. It was difficult for me to know what to expect from him at any given moment. This roller coaster of behavior caused my nerves to constantly be on edge and, with Luke just a few months old and Noah needing constant supervision, I was already stressed. My nerves were so rattled that I couldn't sleep. I felt like I needed to be on watch duty constantly.

However, I knew I had to keep myself together since everyone was depending on me. The only way I could do that was if I calmed down. Since I didn't know how to do that on my own, I called my doctor.

Although I didn't like to admit that I needed help, I could sense myself falling apart. There was no way that I could keep everything together with my anxiety so high. Sadly, my primary care doctor was not helpful. I explained the situation and asked if there was a medication that I could take that would be safe while I was still breastfeeding. I just wanted something that would help me relax a little in moments of high stress. The advice that I received was to stop breastfeeding and take an antidepressant. That was not the answer I was looking for, and I was disappointed. I hadn't taken an antidepressant in years, and I didn't want to take one now. Plus, I didn't want to stop breastfeeding. I would just have to deal with my anxiety on my own.

Upon further reflection and a lot of time spent in prayer, it occurred to me that women often suffer postpartum depression, and I doubted that giving up breastfeeding was part of their prescribed treatment. I figured that there must be safe medication options. Once this realization hit me, I called my obstetrician's office. Sure enough, there was something that I could take that was safe. I had just called the wrong doctor.

The antianxiety medication helped me to calm down on the high-stress days and allowed me to continue caring for everyone's needs. Even though I had been told it was safe, I was still concerned about it passing into my breastmilk. So I was careful to take it only when I really needed it.

At the town meeting, we sat and waited for our project to be discussed. We had hired a consultant to help us in dealing with our town. The town officials didn't want to let us build since the property did not meet typical house lot standards. Our only option was to apply for a variance, attend multiple meetings, perform different tasks, and then hope that the variance would be approved. The consultant was supposed to guide us in this process. Other than being introduced to the consultant, I'd had no dealings with him. Rob had handled the phone calls and had gone with him to the meetings.

I didn't know if Rob had told him about his illness or if the consultant was completely in the dark, but it was hard to hide that something was off with Rob. I can't remember why we were even at that particular meeting, but I remember when the discussion about our property began there was some nitpicking back and forth between the board members and our consultant. As this went on, Rob became agitated. Becoming agitated was not one of his pre-tumor characteristics. Rob had always been an easygoing guy with a calm disposition.

But now he was not himself. I could see his anger brewing as he began to stand up to make his opinion known. I think he was convinced that he would stop the foolishness. A sense of panic engulfed me because I knew that as soon as he opened his mouth, it would be disastrous. He could no longer speak clearly and intelligently. His cancer had stolen that from him, but he didn't even realize it. That was one of the hardest things. He didn't know what was going on. It took some persuading, but I convinced him to stay seated, and the meeting proceeded without incident.

As we spoke with the consultant after the meeting, Rob's condition became evident. To an ignorant eye, it might have appeared as if he was drunk or drugged. It was obvious that something was wrong. I was embarrassed for him. He didn't know how he was appearing, and I was sad that he was not himself.

    I wanted to explain. I wanted to defend him. I wanted to yell out, "He's not drunk! He has a brain tumor!" But I couldn't say anything. I had to pretend that his behavior was normal. He was unaware of his unusual behavior. He deserved to be treated like the man he was, not as a child and not as a patient. I couldn't say anything in front of him. That would have been cruel. Out of respect for Rob, I called that consultant later and told him what was happening. He deserved to know, and Rob's character deserved to not be misconstrued.

CHAPTER 20

Camping and a Kennedy

It was a warm sunny day, and we were sitting on a beach pretending to be normal. To the passerby, we were normal. I don't think anyone could have told by looking at us that anything was wrong. We were just an everyday family spending the weekend camping on the beach.

Regretfully, we weren't normal. Rob was battling a brain tumor, and I was trying to be a loving caregiver for him and a good mom for our two little boys. The clinical trials that Rob's doctor offered him had not helped at all. The tumor was growing. We were in regular contact again with the nutritionist we had consulted with years earlier, and she made recommendations that we hoped would help slow the tumor's growth. Rob's doctor was not optimistic and had no viable treatment options, so we looked for treatment elsewhere. There just had to be something else that he could try.

At first we tried to get an appointment to see a well-known neuro-oncologist whose office was located several states away. We had learned about this doctor at a brain-tumor convention several years earlier. Rob's sister somehow arranged for the doctor to call us, and when he did, he expressed optimism in being able to offer treatment options. Finally, we had some hope again.

Sadly, that hope faded when we could not make an appointment due to the doctor's schedule. It's funny how clerical details like scheduling can affect someone's care. Maybe *funny* is not the right word. *Tragic* is a better word. The expert doctor was willing to treat Rob, but several phone calls to his office staff could not produce an appointment. Since Rob's tumor was growing, time was of the essence. Our only option was to search for another doctor.

This time we contacted a specialist at a hospital in New York City. She agreed to see Rob and begin treatment with the medication that had been effective for him years earlier. She did not share the same views about its potential for effective use on recurrence as Rob's previous doctor. Surprising, she was optimistic, and we both grabbed on to that optimism with everything we had. Now, we just had to get to New York.

Traveling to New York City was like a mini-retreat for us. We didn't have time to explore much of the city, but we enjoyed a delightful meal and a leisurely walk through Central Park. The hospital staff was helpful, and we liked the doctor. She was friendly, caring, and upbeat. We left the city feeling elated that Rob now had a promising treatment plan. Things were looking up.

With everything coordinated remotely by the New York City doctor, Rob began treatment. Some of his odd behavior went away, and there were days when I convinced myself he was getting better. During this time, he expressed his desire to purchase a truck and a camper so we could go camping together as a family. He had owned a camper when I'd first met him, but he'd sold it not long after. I think he regretted selling it because he would often mention going camping. We had gone camping several times with a tent, but that was before we had children.

One time, years earlier, we drove our Jeep to the Adirondack Mountains in New York and spent several days camping in our tent. We would drive to a different location each day, set up camp, and then explore the surrounding area. We hiked, visited historic locations, and fantasized about what it would be like to live in such a beautiful place. As we drove to each location, we would often stop at local restaurants instead of relying on our camping supplies. I really liked that part of our trip. We stopped at a quaint coffee shop one morning and were served fresh-ground coffee in a French press. It was my first experience with coffee prepared this way, and it was delicious!

Now, even though Rob was ill, he decided the time was right to get a camper. We spent weeks searching for a used camper and a used truck to carry it to make this dream of his come true. It became almost an obsession, as it felt like there was an urgency about it. I spent countless hours on the computer searching for exactly what he said we needed. It had to be able to carry a camper on the beach since that was where he wanted to camp.

Purchasing a truck and a camper while we were knee deep in the chaos of cancer seems somewhat foolish when I look back now. We could have just rented something for a weekend away, but I indulged Rob in whatever way I could. How can you say no to the man that you love when he's fighting for his life? Besides that, purchasing something meant he was thinking about the future. He was looking forward to enjoying many camping trips, and that only fueled my delusion that he would get better. His cancer would go away just like before, and we would live a long joyful life as a family.

At last Rob found what he was looking for, and we purchased a truck and a camper. Tragically, by this time Rob's health was getting worse. His speech was slow, and so were his reflexes. His paranoia had decreased, but he was experiencing seizures. His MRI showed some effectiveness of the medication, but not enough to convince his new doctor to continue the treatment. He would need to try something else.

As the days went on, Rob began speaking less and less. I could never tell whether he was choosing to be silent or couldn't make himself speak. Even so, he still wanted to go camping. We packed up what we needed, and I drove us to Cape Cod. Because of Rob's history of seizures, he was not supposed to drive. Having no experience driving a truck with a camper on it would not stop us. We would have our family camping trip to the beach.

Driving on a beach to camp was new to me, so I didn't know what to expect. Fortunately, we would not be alone for most of the adventure. Rob's sister and her family would be there too.

When we arrived, the tires of our dual-wheeled truck had to be partially deflated since that helps you to drive on the beach. Years earlier, when Rob and I would go on off-road rides in his Jeep, he'd followed a similar process with the tires. He knew how to do it. I waited in the truck with the boys while Rob took care of the tires. Then, with Rob's guidance, I followed a path in the sand and parked the truck.

Once we settled our belongings, I plunked down into a beach chair and put my feet in the sand. It was pure bliss to just sit on the beach, forget about everything, and pretend to be normal. With Luke asleep next to me, and Rob's family looking after Noah and Rob, I could finally relax. I was not worried about seizures, paranoia, or inappropriate behavior.

The medication that my obstetrician prescribed was helpful, but what I really needed was a break. My anxiety had been high for months. Every day was a challenge.

Listening to the sound of waves splashing on the shore and feeling the warmth of the sun on my skin took me away for a while. I had no interest in socializing. I was not passing up the opportunity for some quiet time. With a meaningless magazine I did not intend to read, I sat alone and tried my best to think about absolutely nothing. Rob and Noah were perfectly content a short distance away. We would have the rest of the trip together.

Pretending to be a normal family on the beach went well until it didn't. When it was time to leave, we were on our own. Everyone else had left the night before. We secured our belongings in the camper, and I drove slowly along the beach. There were now a lot more tire tracks in the sand than had been there on our arrival. I wasn't sure which tire tracks to follow. Rob attempted to tell me what to do, but I didn't understand what he meant. I chose the wrong path.

With the heavy camper on the back, I attempted to maneuver the truck forward. The tires spun. We were stuck. Surely though, Rob would know what to do. He always knew what to do with things like this. I depended on him for that.

Rob assessed the situation. He tried to advise me as much as he could. Put it in forward, put it in reverse, do this, and do that. Nothing worked.

Rob made some calls to friends and family, but learned that it would take a long time for anyone to come to our aid. We were stranded. In between phone calls and trying to figure out what to do, a couple in a vehicle passed us and then stopped. The man climbed out of his vehicle and asked Rob if he needed any help. Rob was slow to answer. I can't remember if he really answered at all. Rob was trying to deflate the tires. I would learn later that Rob had not deflated the tires upon arrival, at least not to the level that they should have been deflated.

The man tried to ask Rob again if he needed help. I felt bad for the stranger. He was trying to be kind, and Rob was either unable to respond or choosing not to. It was not like Rob to be rude. It was not in his nature. He was a lovable fun guy who would talk with anyone. The tumor had changed him.

I considered speaking to the stranger, but I hesitated. What would I even say? "My husband has a brain tumor and cannot communicate effectively. Yes, we need help." Just like with the town meeting, I couldn't treat Rob like a child. Maybe someone with better social skills could have taken the man aside and discreetly explained the situation. That wasn't me. I didn't know what to do.

Thankfully though, and unbeknownst to us initially, the man did help us. Not long after he drove away, the worker responsible for allowing folks onto the beach drove up. The stranger had let him know about our predicament. He gave us the name of a local towing company that could assist us. He also told us the name of the kind stranger. I wish I could remember the full name. All I remember was that it was someone from the famous Kennedy family. We were told that they were regulars at the beach since they owned property nearby.

We had been clueless about the stranger's identity when he stopped to check on us. We didn't realize he was well known. To me, he was just a kind stranger. It's a shame that he couldn't have interacted with Rob on a better day, when Rob was more like himself. Rob would have enjoyed chatting with him.

It saddens me to think the stranger probably left assuming the worst of Rob. He didn't mean to be rude. I remain impressed by the stranger's character. Despite Rob's rudeness, he helped us anyway. In a sad coincidence, several years later, someone from that stranger's family, Edward Kennedy, was diagnosed and later died from what I believe was the same type of tumor that Rob was battling that day at the beach, the tumor that was stealing my husband away from us.

CHAPTER 21

Writing for my Beloved

Sitting alone in my bedroom with tears in my eyes, I urgently prayed for inspiration. The children were sleeping in the next room, and this was my opportunity, possibly my only chance, to do this one special thing for my husband—I wanted to write him a poem.

Operating out of shock and running only on adrenaline, I had already spent hours rewriting his obituary. The standard text suggested by the funeral home would not do. I wanted it to be exceptional, making sure to include enough information to let the world know just how wonderful he was. I had also worked diligently on the funeral service program and the prayer cards for the wake. I looked at countless examples online before designing my own and sending it off to get printed. My brain was in overdrive. My life had been completely out of control for months, and this was something I could finally control. I had to give all that I could for Rob, and it had to be right. Anything less than my best effort would not be acceptable.

A poem was something much more personal than the other writing I had done thus far. Stubborn willpower and computer skills would not help me. I had to reach into my heart and offer up a piece to honor him. I had to be still, pray that the words would come, and be brave enough to write them down.

Over the last few months, Rob's condition had grown much worse. Nothing helped him. In addition to more seizure activity and odd behavior, Rob almost completely stopped speaking to me, and I was never certain whether he couldn't speak or if he chose not to.

Our social worker advised me to seek services to help with his care. We were fortunate that our health insurance provided for someone to come to our home.

Although it was not obvious to me how dire our circumstances were, I think it was to her. I told myself everything would be fine. Sure, Rob was getting worse, but he would get better just like before. He had to get better. He just needed to find the right treatment and I would help him get well. It didn't matter that I was caring for a sick husband, our baby, and our toddler, plus the household and everything else. I could do it all. I had to do it.

As time went on though, with the social worker's counseling and questioning, I realized that doing it alone meant making impossible choices. I couldn't effectively care for Rob and the children at the same time. The social worker suggested we hire a visiting nurse and a home health aide for Rob, and I made the arrangements.

Although the visiting nurse was not especially kind, Rob didn't seem to mind her. She would check his vitals and ask about his symptoms. Since Rob was still in treatment, hospice services were not available, and she repeatedly made that known to us. We didn't know what services he was supposedly missing out on by continuing to fight his cancer, but I didn't appreciate her attitude. Even if she visited dying patients regularly and considered Rob one of them, in our minds he wasn't terminal. Choosing hospice would have meant giving up all treatment and giving up the fight, and we weren't doing that.

As much as Rob did not mind a visiting nurse, he despised having a home health aide. Around the time when the aide began visiting, his silence grew more prevalent. I think he was mad at me for allowing her to come. What could I do? He had become unsteady on his feet. He could no longer get dressed by himself or get into the shower without help. When I was helping him, the kids went unsupervised, and they were too young for that. I needed help, and he needed help I couldn't give him. I hated that I couldn't do it all. I wanted to give him my full attention, but the kids needed me too.

Even with the help, I still struggled with my responsibilities. At one point, a tenant decided to move out of one of the rental properties, and I had to take over as landlord. Other than typing leases, I had no prior involvement with the tenants. That had been Rob's job. Now, it was mine, and I felt totally unprepared for it. It was so odd to call a stranger and explain the situation. Fortunately, she had been a decent tenant and the moving process went smoothly. Finding another tenant would have to wait. I didn't know then how much I would come to resent the rental properties.

Even as Rob was not himself most days, at times he was fully present. One day when it felt like he was giving up and slipping away, I mustered the courage to pour out my heart to him. I wanted him to know how much the situation scared me and how much I loved him. I wanted him to keep fighting. On that day, in those moments, he spoke to me plainly. Was he still in there and just choosing not to respond all the other times? I was heartbroken and frustrated at the same time.

Then there was the day that we went out to celebrate our wedding anniversary. I don't know why we were still pretending to be normal. Rob had a dental cleaning scheduled that day, and he wanted to keep the appointment. Why was that even important? I didn't know how the appointment would go because he barely spoke and was not acting like himself.

After he went into the dental clinic room, I tried to let the receptionist know about his condition. I thought his hygienist should know what was going on. The receptionist didn't seem to understand what I was telling her, but said she would pass along the information.

To my bewilderment, after the appointment, Rob's hygienist came out to speak with me and mentioned how Rob did fine and how he had told her about our kids. What? I stared at her in disbelief. How could he have told her about our kids? He was not speaking! Was he? I was too shocked and confused to question her. Rob walked out, and the conversation with the hygienist ended. Maybe he had shown her the picture of the boys he kept in his wallet. Maybe he didn't speak and just nodded or grunted responses while she cleaned his teeth. Maybe he actually spoke with her. I'll never know.

We later went out for a celebratory anniversary lunch. I ordered for Rob. Although he wasn't speaking, he would give me a thumbs-up or thumbs-down, with some persuasion on my part. This was how he chose his lunch, with me saying items on the menu and him indicating yes or no with his thumb. It was a pointless lunch. We were going through the motions of celebrating our anniversary just for the sake of it. Why were we even there?

Even as Rob worsened, we were still trying new things that might help him. Having never tried acupuncture before, that was on the list of treatments. At his first visit, the acupuncturist made it clear that acupuncture would not cure Rob, but she suggested it may help with his symptoms. Rob proceeded willingly, but the treatments did not seem to help.

Having tried all the chemotherapy options except for one, we headed back to New York again. This time, one of Rob's sisters came with us. I was thankful because Rob needed constant supervision. He had difficulty walking, and his odd behavior had increased again. The chemotherapy was an intravenous treatment, and I hoped it was the miracle he needed. He made it through the treatment, and we headed back home.

At some point during Rob's illness, we stopped attending church. Rob was not well enough to go, and I couldn't leave him home alone. Frequently, our pastor and assistant pastor would call and visit us. They even started mowing our grass. The pastor's wife and several other ladies took turns helping me with the kids, and many families made us food.

Our families helped too. They would visit or watch the kids while we went to appointments. Or, they would bring us food or other items we needed. It was wonderful to have so many loving and supportive people in our lives. We were living day to day, and I never knew what to expect when I woke up each morning.

The day that my world fell apart began as a splendid summer day. Rob slid out of bed and made it down the stairs to the kitchen by himself. That was unusual, but I took it as a positive sign. Maybe the chemotherapy treatment was working. The days immediately after the treatment had not been good. Rob had refused to eat. As he did not communicate verbally, it was impossible to know if he had an upset stomach or if something else was affecting his appetite or ability to swallow. His doctor assured me it was a normal side effect of the treatment, so I tried not to worry.

As the days went on, he barely ate. If that continued, he would need to be hospitalized. On this morning though, he ate his entire breakfast and took his medication. To me, it was another indicator he was getting better. Maybe he would be all right. Feeling hopeful and lighter for the first time in a long time, I played some music.

For months Rob had insisted on music without words, mostly classical. I don't know why. He had never expressed an interest in classical music before, but on our lengthy rides in and out of Boston, he would always change the radio station to classical music. He refused to listen to songs with words. This morning, though, I wanted to listen to something else, so I played a Randy Travis CD. It didn't last long. I looked over at Rob, and he appeared sad, staring down at Luke crawling near his feet. Thinking the music was too emotional for him, I shut it off.

Another reason that my mood was lighter this day was that I had help on the way. Rob's mom was coming to stay with him and the boys while I went to the photographer to pick up our family photos. Months earlier I had arranged to have our first and only professional family photos taken. Although I thought it was a magnificent idea then, looking at those photos now only brings me pain. Rob's appearance is distorted from the swelling side effect of his medication, and the blank stare in his eyes is haunting. He was there, but he wasn't. On this day, though, I was looking forward to a brief break from my responsibilities at home.

As I tended to the kids and waited for Rob's mom, Rob sat at the kitchen table. What I thought would be a good day immediately took a turn for the worse when Rob's demeanor changed. He appeared to be ill. His head felt warm, and he seemed agitated. By the time his mom arrived, I knew that something was wrong.

Within minutes of her arrival, his behavior grew strange. He attempted to stand and walk to our laundry room. I don't know why. He seemed very concerned about the laundry room. I escorted him to the door and showed him that there was nothing in the laundry room. He didn't seem convinced and tried to open it again.

While walking Rob back to his chair at the kitchen table, he collapsed. Given his history, I thought he was having a seizure. I quickly grabbed his antiseizure medication while instructing his mom to call 911.

Meanwhile, our boys and the two nieces that Rob's mom had brought with her as a surprise were in the other room, oblivious to what was going on. I quickly ran to them, told them to go upstairs, and phoned some family members. We needed help. Rob would most likely be going to the hospital and I wanted to go with him. I couldn't leave Rob's mom with all the kids, and she would probably want to go to the hospital, anyway.

Turning to Rob, I immediately realized something was seriously wrong. He was not moving. I leaned down to him. He was not breathing. Panic filled every inch of my being. CPR. We needed to do CPR. Rob's mom and I took turns, not knowing what we were doing. Rob was unresponsive. Where was the ambulance? Why was it taking so long?

I can't remember how many times we called 911, but I remember the last time. I told the operator that my husband was not breathing. I needed instructions on how to do CPR. To my amazement, the response was "I can't tell you that." I thought I was hearing wrong, so I questioned the operator. "You can't tell me how to do CPR?" When I heard the response "No, I can't tell you that," I hung up the phone. Disgusted that 911 would not help me, I attempted CPR again. Rob remained unresponsive.

It felt like a long time passed before help arrived. The first EMT asked whether Rob had a DNR (do not resuscitate). He didn't. With as much force to my voice as I could manage, I told the rescue workers to revive him. I might have yelled it at them. Maybe that was why someone escorted me outside.

As I waited in the driveway with Rob's mom and a police officer, my mom arrived. Soon after the rescue workers moved Rob into the ambulance. They said I couldn't go in the ambulance, so I planned to follow them in my car. Concerned about my state of mind and my ability to drive safely, my mom asked the police officer whether he thought I should be driving. He graciously offered to bring me and Rob's mom to the hospital. My mom would stay at my house to care for the kids.

I had never been in a police car before, but it felt like the officer was driving slowly. Why couldn't he drive faster? I just wanted to get there. I wanted to be with Rob. Why hadn't they let me ride in the ambulance? I tried to console myself. Rob would get to the hospital, and he would be all right. I was sure that they had revived him already. They must have.

About a half mile before the hospital, I heard some mumbling on the police radio. I thought I heard someone say "D-O-A," but just as I heard it, the officer turned down the radio and spoke to us. He said that the ambulance was at the hospital and that they were working on Rob. I tried to convince myself that he was telling us the truth and that I didn't hear what I thought I had heard. I knew what "D-O-A" meant. No. I must have heard wrong. Rob was at the hospital, and he was fine. He had to be.

At the hospital, a worker led us to a private waiting room. That was unusual, but I tried not to read too much into it. A doctor walked in shortly after and spoke to us. Rob was dead. I couldn't comprehend it. No, Rob couldn't be dead. He was having a good day. He walked down the stairs. He ate his breakfast. He was getting better. He couldn't be dead. Why was this strange doctor telling us this? He was wrong. He must be wrong. Where was my husband?

At some point, other members of Rob's family arrived at the hospital. I can't remember if they came before or after the doctor gave us the news. I remember asking about an autopsy. I wanted to know what had happened. How did he die? What was it on that day that caused his death? Maybe it would help others with his condition. Was it the medication? Was it the supplements? Was it a seizure? I wanted to know what went wrong. Was there something that I could have done to help him? I wanted answers. The doctor told me that an autopsy wouldn't be done, and that was the end of it.

Sitting in that tiny hospital room filled with Rob's family consoling each other, I felt very alone. Unable to fully comprehend that Rob was gone, I sat there dazed and helpless.

At some point our assistant pastor walked into the room and woke me out of my stupor. I found out later that one of Rob's sisters had contacted our church. This man had been a good friend to Rob, and it was immediately comforting to have him there. Not long after, my mom arrived. I didn't know who was taking care of the kids. I knew nothing. I couldn't think.

Someone from the hospital finally asked me if I wanted to see Rob before we left. Of course I wanted to see Rob. My mom walked with me to the room where he was. It was surreal. Looking at Rob lying there on the hospital bed, he could have been sleeping, except he wasn't. He was perfectly still. I spoke to him as if he could hear me. He couldn't. I didn't want to leave. I couldn't just leave him there. It seemed wrong. No, I couldn't leave him there. My mom tried to convince me, but it didn't make sense. I didn't want to leave my husband there. He was supposed to be home with me, with the boys. How could I just leave him there?

Back at my house, the commotion was unbearable. Why were all these people at my house? Maybe it's natural for people to gather and comfort each other, but it didn't seem natural to me. Where were these people when we needed them? I had been mostly on my own for months, caring for Rob, the kids, and everything else. Now, suddenly, everyone could gather at my house in the middle of a weekday. I didn't want to socialize or entertain. I was in shock and I wanted to be alone.

My mom understood my needs and advocated for me. With the house full of people, I retreated on my own to gather my thoughts. I didn't know what to do, but I knew Rob's friends needed to be notified. Rob's friends meant a lot to him, and I didn't want them to read about his death in the newspaper. My mom stepped up again and made the telephone calls. I don't know how she handled everything, because I felt lost and helpless. I didn't even know who was watching my boys, but thankfully someone was caring for them.

After several days of visitors, some of which might have stayed the night, I craved solitude and silence. I wanted everyone to leave me and the boys alone. It was too much. Maybe it made them feel better to be near us, but I didn't understand it. Often it felt like they were seeking comfort from me. I couldn't comfort them. I could barely function. Where were these people when we needed them? Rob was dead. They couldn't help him now. It was too late.

Finally finding a quiet moment to myself, I thought about writing a poem for Rob. Poetry had left my life years earlier, somewhere in the middle of motherhood and caring for a dying husband. I used to find comfort in writing poetry. Putting my feelings into words on a page allowed me to release them from my burdened mind. But this skill, if I can even call it that, had left me, and I wasn't sure if I could get it to come back.

So I sat there on my bed and cried out to the Lord in

desperation. I just had to do this for my husband. It was my special thing, and it was all I could offer. Even though he would never read it, it was something I needed to write. Then the words came. As the tears fell, I scribbled my verses on the page.

For Rob

Hear me, oh Lord
Hear my prayer.
Please welcome my husband
Into your care.

Take his hand,
That I long to hold,
And show him the way.
Let your kingdom unfold.

Reward him fully
For the great things he has done
And the people he touched.
He blessed everyone.

Let him watch over us
In the days ahead.
Let him see how much we love him
How our hearts have bled.

And let us feel his presence
As we keep him ever in mind
And carry his memory
Till the end of time.

Amen

CHAPTER 22

Widow Etiquette

Standing in the cemetery in a loose black dress that draped my disappearing frame, I stared at a fine wooden box, a carefully selected final resting place for my beloved husband. People surrounded me, but I saw no faces. The enormity of the situation was overwhelming. Was it hot or cool, wet or dry? I don't recall. All I remember is that someone was speaking, and I felt weak. My body swayed. My mother and sister moved closer to keep me steady. I wanted to weep loudly. I wanted to fall to the ground and cry out in my grief, but all I could do was stare at that box.

Then it was over. In the most awkward of moments, it was over. What was I supposed to do now? Everyone just stood there, waiting. Waiting ... waiting for what? What was I supposed to do? No one directed me to move. I wanted everyone to leave. At that moment, I wanted to be alone with my dead husband before they buried him in the ground, but I couldn't. Everyone just stood there, probably staring, probably waiting for me to do something. The weight of everyone's expectations was too heavy for me. I couldn't bear the load. I had to do something to make it stop.

So I did. I walked to the casket and said goodbye to Rob and then walked to the limousine. Immediately, I felt like I had done something wrong. What was I supposed to do? Was there proper etiquette for a widow at her husband's funeral? Surely there was some expectation, but I didn't know what it was. I had never been taught how to act at my husband's funeral. I must have missed that information if it was ever given. I slid into the limousine and waited.

Then I watched others say their goodbyes. I had to turn away. It was too much, especially when people took flowers from Rob's casket. Why did they do that? Weren't those Rob's flowers? Maybe it was tradition or maybe it offered some feeling of condolence to the grieving, but I didn't understand it.

The longer I waited alone in the limousine, the more I thought I had done something wrong. Maybe I should have been the last person with the casket. Was that the proper etiquette? Everyone had just stood there waiting for someone to do something. I didn't know what to do. Why didn't someone tell me what to do?

The next thing I remember from this day is being back at our church. The funeral had taken place in the sanctuary before we went to the cemetery. Now we were downstairs in the hall. There were tables with food and tables with people, like a party that nobody wanted to attend.

I sat at a table, unable to function. A few people came up to me, but not many. Maybe I offended them at the cemetery. I didn't know. I knew nothing except that I wanted to go home. It's not that I didn't appreciate all the kind folks who prepared for and had attended this sad event. I did. I was moved by how many people were there. It was just overwhelming, all of it. I couldn't process any of it. My kids were waiting for me to return, and I wanted to see them. They did not understand what was going on. How would I ever tell them?

CHAPTER 23

911 Again

Exactly one week after the Lord took my husband, another emergency emerged. Some family members visited, again. It wasn't that I wasn't grateful to have support, but visits exhausted me. It had been a rough week. After multiple questions from Noah, I had finally gathered the courage to tell him that daddy wasn't coming home. There were many tears shed, even though he didn't fully understand. The week had brought countless phone calls and visits. I didn't want to talk to anyone. I didn't want to see anyone. I knew everyone meant well, but I wanted to be alone. I needed to mourn.

When I was finally alone with my boys, I noticed that Noah felt warm. It had been a busy week for him too, with lots of folks around for playtime distracting. I took his temperature, and it was high, too high. I called his pediatrician's office, and they advised me to give him a dose of children's acetaminophen and a cool bath. This seemed logical, so I followed the instructions and tried not to worry. I was sure he would be fine. Kids get fevers all the time. We had been through so much already. Surely

911 Again

the Lord would not allow for any more stress.

After the bath and the acetaminophen, he felt less feverish. I let him relax on the sofa with some screen time. *Thomas the Tank* was just what he needed, or so I thought. After a few minutes, I looked over in horror. He was shaking all over. I knew that shake all too well. A seizure. I had witnessed Rob's seizures many times.

Immediately, I called 911. I couldn't believe I was calling them, again. I thought I was done calling them. I then phoned my mom ... or my sister. I can't quite remember, but I felt like I needed someone to watch Luke so I could go to the hospital with my shaking child.

The ambulance came quickly, much quicker than the week before. I wondered whether they recognized the address. I wondered whether they came more quickly because they feared the worst. Perhaps they thought I had lost my mind in my grief.

One of the paramedics yelled at me to put a diaper on my child. Having just been in the bath and trying to keep cool, my feverish son was lying undressed on the sofa under a sheet. I didn't know if he meant it, but he yelled in such a way as if to imply neglectful parenting. Shocked and irritated, I stared at him in disbelief. Being potty trained, my son didn't wear diapers anymore. I was not being neglectful. I was trying to keep his temperature down.

Not wanting to argue with the paramedic, I found a diaper I thought might still fit and put it on him. The convulsions had stopped, but he was sleepy. Amid the chaos, someone arrived to take care of Luke, and I went in the ambulance with Noah to the hospital, most likely the same ambulance that I wanted to ride in the week before.

As we rode, a paramedic asked me questions, and I did my best to explain. He looked oddly familiar. I think he had been at my house before. Was he one of the people who had tried to save my husband? Is that why they sought permission to honor my request to go to a different hospital with my son? There was no way I was going back to the same hospital where my husband had been brought.

At the hospital, I faced more questions and procedures. I sat focused on Noah and pretended everything was fine. Unexpectedly, my mother walked into the exam room. Somehow she found me after going to the other hospital first. My sister was caring for the baby. Aside from bringing moral support, she had realized we would need transportation home. I hadn't thought that far ahead, and I was thankful someone was thinking for me. All I could concentrate on was my son.

The next thing I remember is the x-ray room. I don't recall why Noah needed a chest x-ray, but the kind technician realized that my child, still dressed in only a diaper, might be cold and offered me a blanket to cover him. She then instructed me to keep my son still for the x-ray. Keeping a two-year-old from moving might sound challenging, but the Lord gave me a calm song to relax and distract him.

The technician said something afterward like "Good job, Mom." That touched my heart. Thank you, Lord, for that woman. I needed to hear a kind word at that moment. I needed to hear I was a good mom. If she only knew what I had just been through.

CHAPTER 24

The Twenty-Dollar Bill

Sundays became a source of inspiration and a source of frustration. Returning to church after Rob's death took many weeks, but I finally found the will to go back. I'm not sure that I wanted to go, but I felt like I should. So many people in our church had helped me and continued to help me. The least that I could do was show up to church with the boys.

On one Sunday, I sat upstairs in the sanctuary. This was new for me. Usually, I hid downstairs and watched the sermon via telecast with the folks who didn't want to climb up the winding staircase and those who preferred a smaller crowd. It was comfortable downstairs. I could sit in the back away from everyone and let the kids move around without distracting others.

Besides, there were fewer people to see me. I didn't want to be seen. I wanted to crawl into a hole and cry. Part of me felt closer to Rob downstairs, and I so longed to be close to him. Sitting in the room where we used to sit for the evening services somehow brought him back to me a little.

But this was communion day, and for whatever reason, I finally ventured upstairs.

Sitting in the pew with Luke on my lap and Noah beside me, I pretended everything was fine, but it wasn't. I felt out of place and regretted my decision almost immediately, but it was too late to change my mind. I kept my kids occupied with small notebooks and pencils so they could draw quietly and not disturb anyone. I already felt judged for having the kids with me. A nursery and a toddler room were available, and I could have just left them there, as some folks reminded me regularly. Well, I could have left them there if I had wanted to leave them crying and screaming. My kids were not good at being left with others, never mind strangers. I doubt the volunteers would have appreciated me leaving my children in their care. And the boys had been through enough already. Their father had left, and he would never return. They could stay with me at church.

The fussing and the squirming kept my attention away from the pastor. What was he talking about, anyway? What was I even doing there? By the time the serving of communion began, I was exhausted. I was so spent from trying to pretend that I had everything under control. I just wanted to get out of there.

Holding the communion cup of grape juice while trying to keep my wiggling baby still proved to be too much. In a split second, the juice spilled on me, and the attitude in my heart poured out with it. Why did I even think I could pull this off? I was angry, and I let it show. I mumbled under my breath and whined like a child. In that instant, I could have been a cartoon of a bratty little girl stamping her feet with a scrunched-up face and smoke coming out of her ears because she didn't get her way. Of course, I hadn't gotten my way. The Lord had taken my husband and left me to care for two helpless children alone. I was so weak and battered, but I needed to be strong. I didn't want to be strong. I was miserable and angry, and my behavior could not disguise it.

As soon as the service was over, I made my way into the aisle as quickly as possible. Just then a strange thing happened. A woman reached over and handed me something. She said she felt led by the Lord to give it to me. Stunned by the interaction, I thanked her, and she was off. I barely knew this woman. Why was she giving me something?

Outside the sanctuary, I looked down at my hand. A twenty-dollar bill. Why had she just given me a twenty-dollar bill? What did I do to deserve that? I had been whining and complaining. I had acted like a child. Had she been watching me? If so, she must have seen my poor behavior. I was embarrassed just thinking she might have been watching me. I felt guilty. I shouldn't have acted that way. I should have been calm and collected instead of anxious and irritable. Why had she been kind to me? Why had the Lord led her to offer me a gift? I didn't understand it. Even though I was angry with the Lord and let it show, He reminded me I wasn't forgotten. He would provide for us. Even so, I didn't want twenty dollars. I wanted my husband back.

CHAPTER 25

Permission to Destroy

In the days, weeks, and months after Rob's death, some decision or other always demanded my attention. I was responsible for everything. Someone might assume that making decisions alone would be easy, but that wasn't the case. I spent endless hours overthinking decisions. Even after I had chosen a course of action, I second-guessed myself. Maybe I had made the wrong decision. Sometimes, I changed my mind simply because I assumed I had made the wrong decision in the first place.

One decision regarded paying a storage fee. Even though Luke was conceived naturally, we had still maintained the storage of Rob's sperm. We'd never discussed it—not that we had much time for discussions after Luke was born. I didn't know what was left after the IUI attempts, but we had paid an annual fee to keep what was there safely stored.

When the bill for the storage fee arrived, a million scenarios filtered through my head. What if I kept it? Maybe I could conceive again. I could have another piece of Rob. It would be as if a part of him was coming back to me. Another child would give me something else to focus on. By this time I was slipping into depression, and the thought of a baby somehow made sense to my confused mind. I almost had myself convinced it was a marvelous idea.

Then I thought about what Rob would have wanted. Even though he was no longer with me, it would be his child too. He would not have wanted me to bring his child into the world without him. That was one of his greatest fears. He did not want his children to grow up without a father. Of course, the Lord made that decision, anyway.

Rob's intention when he froze his sperm was not for the sperm to be used after his death, but while he was alive. He thought that he would beat cancer, and he had wanted the ability to father his own children. How could I use his sperm without his consent?

Thinking back, there must have been some legal paperwork or something that he signed regarding this issue. But when I contacted the storage facility, I was told it was up to me to decide. Even though my heart longed for another connection to him, I knew he would not have wanted it. Paying to keep that possibility alive was too much of a temptation.

Even now, just thinking about the prospect of giving birth to another of his beautiful children is tempting. I miss the days of caring for my babies. Those days were obscured with grief, and the thought of repeating them in a better state of mind is appealing. There's a part of me that still longs for this so much that it physically hurts. I wish I could go back and change my mind, even if it would have been the wrong decision.

But I loved him too much to go against his wishes,

even if he'd never told me those wishes directly. I knew in my heart what the right thing to do was, and that was not to keep the sperm. I called the facility and they sent me a form to sign. When it arrived, I panicked as I read the words across the page, "permission to destroy." Destroy? The word pierced me. It sounded awful. I didn't want to give permission to destroy. I wanted to hold on to him forever, even if it was just an infinitesimal part of him frozen away, never to be seen again. It took me an agonizingly long time to sign that paper and send it back, but I finally did it. It hurt so much to let go of him again.

CHAPTER 26

The Merry Helpers

Standing at my kitchen sink, I methodically uncorked each bottle of wine and poured the bubbly liquid down the drain. I didn't think about the wastefulness of my action. I didn't think about how much money I had spent on that case of wine. All I could think about was the fact that I needed to get rid of it before anyone saw it. The merry helpers would arrive soon.

Drinking wine had long since left my daily routine, but there was a time when it brought me comfort at the end of the day. After Rob's death, I spent many evenings drinking a glass of wine or two. It was my reward for making it through another day. Since my body had stopped producing breastmilk after Rob's death, I was no longer breastfeeding. Nothing prevented me from having a glass of wine in the evening.

Taking care of the boys while mourning the loss of my husband had taken its toll. Mourning was not exactly what I was doing. I was sinking into a pit of despair. I looked forward to my wine. I needed that wine, or so I thought. I didn't overindulge, at least not by society's standards, and

I would wait until I settled the boys in the evening. Baths and story time came first. Then I relaxed in front of the television with my bubbly remedy.

I can't count the number of times the Red Sox kept me company on those evenings. I knew all the players, their batting styles, who had injuries, and what team they were playing next. I was not much of a sports fan, nor had I ever been one, but the baseball games kept my mind distracted during those gloomy days. A glass of wine and a Red Sox game became my nightly ritual.

Although I attempted to function each day, it was becoming increasingly difficult, and I knew I needed help. I also wanted professional support for my children. Being an excellent mom had become my primary goal, and that meant not ignoring the impact of Rob's death on the mental health of the boys. So I sought services from a counselor who worked with children and adults.

To my relief, the counselor was pleasant, optimistic, and helpful. The boys liked her too. I appreciated that she gave me practical strategies for dealing with different situations. It wasn't like before, when counselors focused primarily on me being damaged from my past, or the social worker who'd focused on dealing with Rob's illness. This counselor focused on identifying my present-day needs and meeting those needs. She taught me how to take positive steps in my new role as a widowed mom.

Regrettably, she was also a strong supporter of medication. Although I had taken antidepressants several times before, they'd never produced positive results. I don't think the chemicals in my brain were ever the actual issue, or if they were, the medicines didn't alter them as intended.

This time I didn't give in to medication, at least not at first. Agreeing to medication would mean the end of my nightly wine routine. Alcohol and antidepressants did not mix well, and I did not want to give up my wine.

I had begun ordering it online by the case because it was less expensive and more inconspicuous. I didn't have to worry about running into someone from our church at the grocery store with a bottle of wine in my cart. Even though I was not drinking in excess, I was still concerned that it would be perceived wrong. I did not want anyone to question my judgment or ability to mother my children. I had to be careful. I was responsible for two precious lives, and I did not take that responsibility lightly. No one was going to take my children away.

About two bottles into my last case of wine, I felt like God told me to stop. It was as if someone said, "You've had enough. It's time to knock it off." So I stashed away the rest of the case, gave up drinking, and sank deeper into my black pit of grief.

With each day that passed, I felt more lost than the day before. I looked to books to help me. Reading about the stages of grief was a joke. I did not fit in any stage, and even if I did, I couldn't see how that could help me. The only thing that I wanted was my husband, and he wasn't coming back.

For a time, I became fixated on afterlife communication. Still young in my faith, I didn't know about the dangers of false teachers. I was desperate to hear from my husband and became preoccupied with a man on television who claimed to have supernatural powers and the ability to hear from the dead. Thankfully, God opened my eyes to the deception of the television personality when I attended one of his in-person events. Although I was disappointed, I was almost relieved to escape that slippery slope of darkness.

With no more wine and no more afterlife obsessions, I became convinced that the only thing that could help me was medication. Besides, I was clinically depressed. I had all the symptoms. Plus, I had anxiety. I was broken, and medication would fix me, even though it hadn't before. I just had to find the right pill or combination of pills. So my counselor arranged for me to see a psychiatrist.

As my psychiatrist experimented with different medications, my counselor had her own arsenal of therapies. Sometimes I would bring Noah to appointments to gauge how he was coping with the loss of his dad. My counselor had storybooks about feelings and games about emotions. Seeing how well my son interacted and responded was comforting. He was fine. Later, I brought Luke too. Other times when it was just me, we did visualization exercises. I remember one so clearly, it hurts.

Is it possible to miss the memories you never had? I do. I miss the memories that Rob and I could have made together. My counselor had me do a visualization exercise that was supposed to help with my anxiety. She had me breathe slowly, close my eyes, and then imagine myself sitting in an empty movie theater. Then I was to picture myself getting up and walking through a big blank screen. Then I was to picture myself standing in an empty hallway with some doors. Each door I passed would be locked with a sign on it that read something like "Worries about my children. Closed. Do not enter." There would be several locked doors, each with different stress-inducing items posted on them and each stating that I couldn't enter. Then I would get to a door with no sign, open the door, and walk through the doorway. I was supposed to imagine that all the things that made me happy and peaceful were in this room. I was to walk in and experience the wonderful imaginary room.

Even though we did this exercise many times, I always imagined the same special room. I can still picture this fantastic place. I walk into a solarium filled with all sorts of beautiful plants and wild birds. There's even a fountain, and I can hear the soft trickling water. The sun shines a comforting light through the glass panels. The air is warm and moist, and the sweet floral aroma is intoxicating. At the far end of the room, big glass doors are open to the outside. I can see the green grass and my boys playing on it. I take a seat on a padded bench and relax in the solarium.

After a bit, one of my boys comes in and beckons me outside. This is the part that always gets me. I stroll outside, and I notice that it's not just my kids playing. Rob is with them. He's pushing them on a swing and running around with them in the sunshine. They all have huge smiles and are perfectly content. I allow myself to be content too, completely absorbed in this blissful moment. The world is as it should have been.

Then I hear my therapist telling me it is time to open my eyes. Reluctantly, I leave my happy world and come back to reality. Sadness returns.

This is what I miss. I miss the chance to experience simple moments with my husband and kids. I miss being able to look over at his smiling face as he pushes our kids on the swings. I miss sharing a beautiful sunny day. For many years, when I was feeling brave, I would go to that imaginary world on my own just to experience what I missed. It was a temporary peacefulness. I traded a few minutes of pure tranquility for tears. I would always come back to a pain that hollowed my heart. I don't go to that imaginary place anymore. My heart needs healing, not punishment.

Maybe it was the medication or maybe it was the counseling, but over time I began to contemplate my living situation and pondered my options. I didn't want to stay in our current house. We were never supposed to live in that house long term, and there were too many negative memories. There was not a single room that I could go to without remembering a terrible incident that had happened there. There was the top of the stairs, where Rob had a seizure. There was the living room, where I had to install dark blinds because Rob thought there were people lurking outside. There was the bathroom, where he thought someone was hiding. The list went on and on. Then there was the kitchen, where he spent his last breaths before dropping to the floor.

I didn't want to stay in the house. I considered looking for another house to purchase, but I felt guilty about that. What about our dream house? We had already gone through the permit process, and at some meeting that we didn't attend during Rob's illness, the town had finally approved it. The permission to build was finally available if I wanted to accept it, but did I want it?

Starting over with an existing house somewhere else was probably the most logical step, but I was not in a logical state of mind. I was depressed. Somehow, the thought of building the house we'd planned made more sense. I felt like I owed it to Rob to go through with the project. That building a house would be difficult did not even enter my mind. How hard could it be? After everything I had been through, building a house had to be easier.

As usual, I started with research, reading whatever I could find about building your own home. The thought of hiring a contractor to oversee the entire project would probably have made sense to most people, but not to me. Rob was supposed to be that person, and I couldn't bring myself to fill that role with anyone else. Plus, that would have meant an added expense that we had not budgeted. I read a book that described how to act as your own contractor. It made it sound easy, and I became convinced I could do it. Looking back now, it was not the best decision.

Months later, I read some advice about not making any major life decisions for a full year after a loved one dies. That's excellent advice, and I wish I had followed it. I was in no state of mind to take on the project, never mind act as my own contractor. What was I thinking? I wasn't thinking. I was looking for something to keep me from thinking. It was easier not to deal with my grief.

Building the house would be an excellent distraction, and I rationalized that it would give me something to look forward to. Really, I was looking for another way to connect with my husband. In my mind, building the house would somehow honor him. Cancer may have taken him, but it was not taking his dream home. So, besides battling an ever-increasing level of anxiety and depression, I decided to build a house.

It seemed like a splendid idea. I would use my research skills to scope out deals and build the house as inexpensively as possible. We had already obtained a building loan before Rob's illness, so all I had to do was stay within my budget. That was very important because I was becoming increasingly fearful of spending. The multifamily rental properties were not a reliable source of income, and I did not want to have to go back to work. I wanted to stay home with the boys. So I had to be careful.

With encouragement from family and friends, I went all in. My brother-in-law stepped up to help, completing various projects along the way so I didn't have to hire them out. It was exciting to walk with the boys to the building site to see the progress. I didn't know what to expect, and I did not appreciate the scale from the blueprints. To this day, I don't know what Rob was thinking. The house was huge. It was beautiful, but it was large, much too big for a single mom and two little boys. I tried not to think about that. I was building Rob's house. I needed to build it, and we would live in it just like we were supposed to. I remember a few subcontractors remarking about me having to clean and take care of the place. I just brushed those comments aside. I could do it. What did they know? I could do it. It would be fine. How foolish and smug I was.

With the house underway, I spent my days caring for the boys and dealing with contractors. Once each week, one of the merry helpers, as some of them liked to be called, would watch the boys for a few hours. These were ladies from church who had first offered to help me when Rob was sick and then continued to do so throughout his illness and long after he was gone. The pastor's wife, who established the helpers, and the other ladies, each took turns spending time with the boys so I could have a break.

The Merry Helpers

I typically used the time to get things done around the house. It's amazing how productive you can be when you are not worrying about your little ones.

One of the ladies watched the boys at her home. On those days I would usually indulge myself with a take-out coffee and some shopping. I don't know where I would be now without those ladies. Not only did they provide another loving person for my boys, but their visits helped my mental state enormously. I could get through the worst day if I knew someone was coming that week to help me. Not only that, but I also had to keep my act together. Knowing that someone is coming to your home tends to make you want to make it presentable. My house was not super tidy, but I'm positive that I would have completely neglected it and myself if I hadn't had a reason to try. The visits helped keep me accountable. The ladies also chatted with me, and I always felt better afterward. I didn't feel like I deserved their kindness, but they gave it anyway. They were such a blessing to me and the boys, and I am so thankful for them.

Pouring out the wine in my kitchen sink that day, I felt a sense of relief when the bottles were empty. They were no longer there to tempt me, and no one would know about them. The merry helpers and several others came that day to help us. It was moving day. A new chapter of our lives was about to begin. The house was finally ready, and our family was moving in, without Rob. It felt wrong.

CHAPTER 27

No More School

Standing in the office supply aisle at Target with Luke sitting in the shopping cart and Noah by my side, we embarked on our first homeschool lesson and field trip. This was a test. This was only a test. Could I provide daily educational opportunities for my kids? Was I crazy to think this was a good idea?

Days earlier, I had mailed a letter to our local elementary school withdrawing my three-year-old from preschool and my five-year-old from kindergarten. Noah had attended preschool part time for two years and done well. He'd enjoyed it. Kindergarten was different. Within a few weeks, he went from being a happy and engaged young child to a stressed, emotional teenager in a five-year-old's body. I don't think it was one particular event that caused this change. Rather, it was a combination of factors that came together and stole my little boy.

As for Luke, we tried preschool. He did not take well to being left with strangers, even for a few hours. He was supposed to have the teacher and aide that Noah had for two years. Luke had grown accustomed to seeing these two women regularly when we'd dropped off and picked up his brother. I think he would have been comfortable with them. However, the aide left before the start of the school year, and the lead teacher had some sort of emergency and was absent most days.

So two strangers took over the class, and this did not bode well for my son. He cried and screamed every time I left him. I found out later that his screaming at drop-off resulted in him losing playground time at recess. I guess that was the teacher's form of punishment for screaming, and it was supposed to result in stopping the behavior. It didn't.

Homeschooling had never been on my radar. I had gone to college to be a teacher and fully supported the traditional school model. I knew nothing about homeschooling except that one of my neighbors did it. It just so happened that around the time I was becoming uneasy with my sons' schooling that my neighbor invited us for dinner. She gladly filled me in on homeschooling and on the fact that kindergarten was not even mandatory in our state. I didn't know that. I had just assumed that I should send Noah to kindergarten. I didn't even realize that I had a choice. My neighbor sent me home that night with some interesting reading material about the educational system and homeschooling. Maybe I had a choice after all.

A lot of prayer and tons of research occurred before I took the plunge and sent that withdrawal letter. I almost didn't send it. I considered just withdrawing Luke from preschool and asking if I could switch Noah from full-day kindergarten to part day. There were two programs, and I had chosen the full day because I thought it would be better. There was no doubt in my mind that the preschool class was not right for Luke, but the decision about kindergarten would take more time.

My resolve to homeschool was finalized in my mind the day I called the school to discuss Noah's reaction to kindergarten. I can't recall who I asked to speak with first. I kept asking for different people who I thought might offer some insight, and no one was available to speak with me. No one. The secretary told me no one was available to speak with me regarding my concerns. How could no one be available to speak with a parent? I was eerily reminded of that 911 call when I was told that they couldn't help me. I made my decision. The boys would stay home.

My plan was to homeschool for one year. We had become more actively involved in our church, and both boys were interacting with other children regularly, so I was not concerned about socialization. Academically, Noah had already mastered many of the skills he supposedly needed for his grade level. I remember at one of the parent-teacher conferences with his preschool teacher that she remarked that I must have been working with him at home. I recall just staring at her because I was confused by her statement. We didn't "work" on things at home. We played games, sang songs, solved puzzles, read stories, and enjoyed fun things together. Sure, he was constantly learning throughout the day, but I thought that's what kids were supposed to do. I thought part of being a mom was doing these things, and I just assumed that everyone did them. Evidently not.

Walking around Target that day I found that not only did I enjoy turning a shopping trip into an educational experience, I felt a renewed sense of purpose. The passion I used to have when learning how to be a teacher was rekindled. Maybe I wasn't an early education specialist, but I knew how to teach and design lessons. We had just moved into our new house, and it felt like the timing was right for this fresh adventure for all of us.

Over the next few days, I performed research, gathered supplies, and planned the rest of the school year. Before long, both my children were thriving at home, with my oldest son returning to his former self. I was so thankful to have him back.

CHAPTER 28

A Mom and her Backhoe

Sitting in the driver's seat, if it's even called that, with a small child on either side of me, I carefully maneuvered the backhoe. I was attempting to lift a bat house and hang it from the top of the pole that I had installed in our yard. I'm not sure which is more ridiculous, a mom operating large machinery with two little ones assisting her or someone using a backhoe to install a bat house.

This was no ordinary bat house. I had done extensive research about bat houses. According to the experts, it had to be a particular size with certain specifications and constructed with nontoxic materials. I wanted to have the right type of house for our bats. I did not know when I ordered it that it would be handmade and would take weeks to arrive. I also did not realize how heavy it would be or how high I would need to hang it. My eight-foot ladder would not work, as it was too short. I was also not strong enough to hold it by myself and mount it at the same time. So using the backhoe seemed like a logical idea to a homeschooling mom on a mission.

Hanging the bat house would be the culminating activity of our homeschool study on bats. I can't recall which grades my sons were in then. After our first year of homeschooling, we never looked back because homeschooling just seemed to fit our family. The freedom of the lifestyle suited us well. I loved researching ideas for lessons and developing unit studies for different topics that involved activities in multiple subject areas. A basic textbook was not enough. I could do better than that, and I continually pushed myself to do so.

The early days of homeschooling were filled with many fun learning adventures and projects. We went on interesting field trips and attended homeschool outings with other families, but the days were not easy. It was difficult to be a single mom and a teacher. Many tasks that I would have been able to complete, if the boys had been in school, went undone. Basic housekeeping and simple meals were all I could accomplish. The boys helped with a few chores. When I knew company was coming, I raced to clean our home to make it more presentable, all the while irritated with myself for building such an ambitious house and for not being able to care for it properly.

To maintain my sanity and the overall health of our family, I kept bedtimes and mealtimes consistent and avoided extracurricular activities that could potentially interfere with them. This meant saying no to things often.

For the unit study on bats, we read stories, watched videos, and completed writing, geography, science, and art activities. We learned about the many benefits of different species of bats, and this sparked the idea to install a bat house. Our bats would be happy in their new home and voraciously eat all our mosquitoes. It would be perfect. We just had to get the bat house installed.

As strange as it may seem, riding in the backhoe was nothing new for my kids. I had taken them on many slow rides around our property—always a fun event. What little boy doesn't enjoy riding in a gigantic machine? After Rob died, I used the machine many times. Moving dirt and scraping the gravel driveway became part of my kid-free time. I thought I was fairly skilled at operating the machine until the day I misjudged how close I was to my car and smashed the rear light.

Purchasing and using the backhoe had been such a highlight for Rob. He had been so excited the day he came home from the equipment auction. Like I said, what little boy doesn't enjoy riding in a gigantic machine? One of my favorite photos is of him with an enormous smile on his face, operating that backhoe. He loved that thing. Perhaps that was why I held onto it for so long. Or maybe it was because he always talked about what a brilliant investment it was. He said we would get so much use out of it, that over time it would pay for itself. Or maybe it was because I had neither the knowledge nor the energy to sell it. Just the thought of it was overwhelming.

Rob had me ride with him in the machine several times and even taught me how to operate it. I think he enjoyed teaching me things, as he taught me many things. I'm not sure if that proved to be a blessing or a curse, because it gave me the idea that I could do things that I wasn't qualified to do instead of seeking help.

Installing the bat house was proving to be problematic. I could not see well enough to get it on the pole, but, being stubborn, I still tried to get it done. At some point I decided it was a good idea to have Noah stand on the ground in view of the pole and verbally guide me.

Upon seeing my son standing there, my brain panicked, and fear enveloped me. I stopped the machine. What was I doing? I was putting faith in my skills as a backhoe operator to move heavy equipment near my child. I was not a backhoe operator! Even if I was one, it was a foolish idea. Noah was safely out of range of the machine, but what if I accidentally moved forward or incorrectly moved a lever? He was not far enough away for mistakes.

What was I thinking? Our homeschool study would be ruined, and I would be a failure, again. That was what I was thinking. Full of guilt for placing my unrealistic expectations ahead of common sense, I put an end to our installation. Relieved that my son was fine but disappointed with myself, I felt defeated. Why couldn't Rob be here to help me? Why did God have to take him? Why did I have to do everything alone? Rob would have installed that bat house in minutes and done it well. For me, everything was a struggle, and I was so tired of doing it all by myself.

That bat house never got installed. It's still sitting in my basement and has taunted me for years, reminding me of my failure. Looking back now, it should remind me that God opened my eyes that day to the potential danger of the situation and kept us all safe. I know that in my head, but sometimes lies lead my heart astray.

CHAPTER 29

The Widow's Curse

Standing with a group of homeschool moms while our respective children played on the grass nearby, I reluctantly listened as the women discussed their husbands' attitudes toward homeschooling. Secretly hoping no one would notice that I wasn't taking part in the conversation, I smiled and nodded when it seemed appropriate.

Why did they have to talk about their husbands? Idle chitchat was hard enough to make any sense of, but they had chosen a topic to which I couldn't contribute. I desperately wanted to fit in with these ladies. My kids needed a sense of normalcy, and the regular meetings of this homeschool cooperative provided that. The boys also needed a place to fit in and form friendships with other homeschoolers. I needed to fit in so that they could fit in, but I didn't know how to fit in.

After several minutes of listening, I realized I was the only mom who had said nothing. What could I say? I barely knew these women, and I didn't want them to know my story. Being socially awkward, quiet, and shy was bad enough. Admitting I was a widow would distance me even more. I just wanted to appear as an average homeschool mom. Maybe someone would change the topic. *Please, someone, change the topic.*

Even though she likely had the best of intentions, one mom noticed I hadn't contributed and questioned me to bring me into the conversation. Uh-oh. I was caught. Now what?

Knowing full well the reaction it would elicit, but having no other option, I gently admitted my widowhood to the group of moms. Silence. There it was, the widow's curse.

Losing my husband was torture enough, but I was not prepared for the other ramifications, those painful interactions that I came to label as the widow's curse. No one wants to know that you're a widow. Admitting that you're a widow is admitting that life is fragile. No one likes to face that. No one wants to be reminded that death does not discriminate. No one wants to think about the possibility of losing their spouse. Since I was a reminder of that possibility, people behaved differently around me when they found out I was a widow. I don't think they meant to, but they did it anyway. I was the ominous cloud in their imaginary sunny sky. If I wasn't already lonely enough, knowing that my presence elicited unpleasant feelings in others made me even lonelier.

Sometimes people tried to compensate for my loss by showering me with compliments or sympathy. Some people insisted on paying for meals or other things. In the beginning, this seemed like an acceptable practice, but as it continued, it felt wrong. Although I was thankful for the kindness, treating me like a charity placed confusing barriers in relationships. I never knew where I stood with people who behaved like this. Were they just being kind because I was a widow, or were we really friends? If we were friends, then why not treat me like an equal? If someone insisted on paying repeatedly, I didn't know if I should continually interject or just let them pay. This confusion made me feel worse about myself.

The widow's curse goes beyond feeling like a dark cloud or a charity. Over time I learned that part of the widow's curse was dealing with the misconstrued ideas of others. Sometimes people acted like I was a threat. My singleness and seemingly financial security became obstacles to true friendship. I remember when someone complained that her husband said something complimentary about me. She was mad about it. I supposed she was jealous, but it made no sense. Why would she be jealous of me? Her husband was alive and supporting her family. I was alone and struggling. Why would anyone be jealous of me? Some women did not seem to appreciate it if I spoke to their significant others or if their significant others spoke to me. I think they saw me as a single woman and as a threat. This was ludicrous, since I was still devoted to my dead husband.

Sometimes it was the husbands who treated me strangely. I suspect my independence was intimidating. Maybe they feared that their wives would prefer to be on their own like I was. Maybe they thought I'd corrupt them and convince them that singleness was better.

I had a friend who often complained about her husband to me. I tried to be supportive and listen, but it was painful because she would often throw daggers in the conversation by implying I was better off since I didn't have to deal with marital issues. She did not understand what I was going through or how wrong she was.

After admitting to the homeschool moms that my husband was dead, the heavy silence was too much to bear for the woman who had invoked the response. She offered some condolences and praise to clear the air, but the damage was done. I felt like a wall had been built around me. No longer was I just another homeschooling mom; I was the widow. Some brave souls asked me later how I supported our family. Admitting that I owned rental property added another brick to my wall. Most of the moms did not work. They relied on their husbands. If they only knew about the depression and the anxiety, then I would be completely closed off. Maybe I already was.

With my wall firmly built, I never felt like I fit in. I tried to be helpful within the group, but I felt out of place. Lacking the skill of small talk, I stumbled in conversations. Often, I found it easier to keep to myself. I prayed that my boys wouldn't suffer because of my inadequacies. Living without their dad was suffering enough.

CHAPTER 30

Shrinking into Nothingness

Trying to control my frustration, I swallowed hard when the doctor tossed her accusation at me. She began with questions. What was I doing there? What did I expect her to do? What did I eat that day? Being the anxious woman I was, I did my best to answer without too much hesitation.

What was I doing there? That one baffled me. She should have known why I was there. My primary doctor was concerned about my weight loss and wanted a hematologist to assess me. My doctor, through an exam and several blood tests, had found nothing to indicate what was causing the weight loss. Maybe the hematologist wanted to make sure I knew why I was there, but the tone in which she questioned me made it seem like I was deliberately wasting her time. What did I expect her to do? Well, I expected her to use her expertise to figure out if I had an underlying condition.

What did I eat that day? Surprised by the question, it took me a minute to answer. What had I eaten, and why was she even asking me that? I knew I'd eaten something, since I always ate. Then I remembered that I had been rushing to get to the appointment on time and had purchased a bagel and a coffee on the way there. Maybe it wasn't the most nutritious meal, but I didn't think it was too bad or unusual.

Following this question, there were several more about my diet before I realized what she was up to. She was accusing me of not eating, of intentionally losing weight. I was livid. Why on earth would I waste my time going to doctors, arranging for childcare each time, and subjecting myself to repeated blood draws to find out why I was losing weight if I was doing it on purpose? I might have been anxious, depressed, and not sleeping, but I was not trying to lose weight. Besides, my primary care doctor had sent me there. It wasn't my idea. I didn't even want to be there!

I left the office mad and completely defeated, like a little child who had been scolded. I was eating. I loved to eat. I ate whenever I was hungry, and that should have been enough, but it wasn't. Other than playing games outside with the boys or going for walks with them, I wasn't exercising. Exercising was the last thing that I wanted to do. Why was I losing weight? Something was going on with my body. I was shrinking.

Months earlier, I had been switched to a different psychiatrist. It was at one of our first visits that she said to me, "You seem a little slow." She was referring to my energy level, and she was right. I was slow. Trying to care for my boys and our home and the rental properties by myself was exhausting. Plus, I wasn't sleeping well. Often, I would lie awake for hours because my anxiety level was so high. My primary care doctor suggested a prescription sleeping pill, but I declined. How could I do that? I was the only adult in our home with two little boys. I couldn't take medication that would knock me out.

My therapist had suggested I practice deep breathing and listen to calming music at night. I wasn't sure if this would work, so I performed a test. I counted my pulse before playing the music. Then after several minutes of deep breathing and focusing on the music, I counted my pulse again. It was always lower. Even though I wasn't sure if this meant I was more likely to fall asleep, I figured it might help. So night after night, I listened to the music and focused on my breathing. Many nights I still didn't sleep well, but I relaxed a little.

At the time of my sluggishness, I was taking an antidepressant or two. It might have been making me slow. I don't remember which one I was taking then. I had tried so many because my former psychiatrist was never satisfied with the results. However, this was the first time a psychiatrist looked at me carefully and then verbalized my demeanor. Not only that, she genuinely seemed like she wanted to help me. Her suggestion was to add another medication to my daily regimen to address my energy level.

At first it was great. The added medication gave me a little boost to get through the day. I had more energy to play with the kids and get things done around the house. I felt better. However, the boost lasted into the evenings and added to my sleeping problem. The calming music did not stand a chance against a stimulant. The answer to the sleeping problem was to add another medication to the mix. Since I didn't want something so strong that it would knock me out, my psychiatrist prescribed the antianxiety medication that I had taken during Rob's illness.

So my days consisted of taking antidepressants to supposedly help with my depression, a stimulant to help my energy level, and then a depressant to help me sleep. At some point the stimulant made me jittery, so I decreased the dosage. This daily dose of pills went on for months.

The weight loss was gradual at the beginning and then suddenly ramped up. Before I knew it, I had dropped from a size ten to a size two. I was thinner than I had ever been as an adult.

Since the hematologist found nothing to indicate an underlying condition that would cause weight loss, I wondered if it was the combination of medications. Maybe my body was processing the drugs differently than before. Now what was I supposed to do? The stimulant helped my energy level. What would happen if I decreased it or stopped taking it? I didn't want to go back to being lethargic. I enjoyed the energy boost. I finally felt productive, and my overachiever mind relished it. I had even become more social, taking a more active part in church activities and with the local homeschool group. My introverted self hadn't changed, but I was getting out more. According to my therapist, getting out more would help fix me. I needed the medication to do all the things I was supposed to be doing.

Plus, part of me liked being thin. I had never been overweight, but I had experienced weight gain off and on over the years from the different antidepressants and from poor eating habits. Now, I could eat whatever I wanted and not gain weight. Ice cream every day was not a problem. My clothing never felt tight, and I liked it.

Besides, I didn't think I was too skinny. I was fine. Maybe I didn't need to do anything at all. Maybe it was just the trauma with the loss of my husband and the stress of trying to handle everything alone that was causing my weight loss. I decided to do nothing.

God quickly put an end to that plan.

CHAPTER 31

A Cookout Casualty

I was in good spirits that morning. We had plans. We actually had plans. We had been invited to a friend's cookout, and I had agreed to go. I had even volunteered to bring food. My therapist would be happy with me. I would get out of the house with the kids and actively engage in a social environment, something I didn't do often and something I usually dreaded. It would be a splendid day.

I prepared a salad and a dessert. My friend had asked me to bring the salad, but that wasn't enough for me. I had to bring a dessert too. The kids played contently in another room while I worked in the kitchen. All was well.

Then I was trying to be fancy with the vegetables. Simple chopping would not do. A mandolin had to be used for this salad, since I wanted it to look especially nice. This device was a recent purchase, and I had only used it once or twice. I had such high hopes. I would slice the cucumbers with the mandolin, and the salad would look great. Besides, I had convinced myself that it wasn't a decision made from pride but of practicality. It would be much more efficient to slice them this way.

As I began, I was careful to keep my fingers away from the blade. Yet, I was not careful enough. It happened so quickly that I didn't even feel it at first. The blood from my finger put an immediate end to my salad making.

I dashed to the bathroom to get a bandage, my head spinning. Bleeding was not something that I handled well, and fainting was my usual reaction.

I don't think it's the blood itself that is bothersome; it is the idea that the flow of blood is unstoppable and completely out of my control. Just thinking about it now is making me dizzy.

I could not faint. I had to calm down. *Breathe in, breathe out.* After a few minutes of deep breathing, I applied some strong bandages.

Thankfully, I dealt with the situation without alarming the boys, and there was no fainting this time. Convincing myself that the cut wasn't too deep, I went back to my cooking. Even when I had soaked through the bandage only minutes later, I pretended all was well. I replaced the bandage and made it even tighter. We had plans, and nothing would stop us.

At the cookout, I tried my best to join in. Social gatherings were often akin to punishment in my mind, but I was trying to enjoy myself. It was a very warm summer day, and I became more and more uncomfortable sitting outside in the sun with the other adults. Some children, including my own, were playing in the shade, so I nonchalantly walked over and chatted with them. Not surprisingly, they had no interest in my chitchat and left the area for more exciting things. I felt a little better standing in the shade, but my finger started throbbing.

I don't know how long I stood there alone, but at some point I noticed that the other adults were looking at me. Thinking about it now, I'm sure it looked odd for me to be standing away from them by myself. I tried to go back to the others, but the heat was unbearable and the throbbing in my finger had turned into pain. I had to get out of the sun. I couldn't understand why no one else seemed bothered. The heat felt so intense.

Hoping no one would notice, I walked around the house and hid in the open garage. I could have just gone inside the house, but the party was outside and I didn't want to be rude to our hosts. Plus, I was confused, and sitting alone in the garage seemed like the best option.

I can't even remember who found me, but the next thing I remember is being told to lie down on a couch inside.

I looked up to see our host, a friend from church who was coincidently a nurse, and told her about the cut on my finger. After that, my body betrayed me. I'm not sure if I had a panic attack, but something happened. My breathing went crazy and my mind went with it. I began thinking about my boys and wondering who would care for them if I was no longer able to. I thought about the families at the cookout and pondered which one would be the best fit. It all played out in my mind like I had to make an immediate decision and choose the best person present to be my substitute.

I don't know if it was the injured finger, heat, medication, weight loss, grief, or the combination of all of it that sent me over the edge. It might have been the fact that I wasn't feeling well and someone was there to take care of me. Maybe God chose that moment to let me lose control because someone else was there to be in control. I don't know, but it was frightening.

During all of this, I looked up and saw my kids looking in the window at me lying there. Seeing those two little concerned faces brought me back to reality. They were worried about me, and I had to get my act together for their sake. They needed me.

The rest of the cookout was a blur. I was thankful that my friend had taken care of me, but I was embarrassed that I had lost control. I tried to act as if nothing had happened, but there was a noticeable awkwardness in the air. Despite my discomfort, we stayed for some time since the boys were having fun playing with the other kids. I didn't want to make them leave on my account. It was a relief when we finally got home. After putting the boys to bed, I could take a pill, go to sleep, and try to forget about the day.

CHAPTER 32

A Bible Study Revelation

I didn't know what to expect that morning. A new women's Bible study was being offered for the ladies of our church during the Sunday school hour, and it had something to do with a book about not feeling well. I had not felt well in years, so I decided to try it. The boys were regularly attending Sunday school classes on their own, so I had the freedom to join an adult study.

As I walked into the room, I looked for familiar faces. I suspected I was the youngest one there. Uh-oh. Maybe I had made the wrong choice. I was overcome with even more anxiety than I already had and felt trapped. I couldn't escape the room unnoticed, but I wasn't sure if I should stay. Trying to stay calm, I sat down and waited for the leader to begin. After a brief introduction, it was time for awkward questioning. We took turns stating our names and telling everyone why we were there. When it was my turn, I mentioned to this group of older women, ladies I didn't know on a personal level, that I had suffered from anxiety and depression for years.

There. I said it. It lingered in the air like an unpleasant

aroma. No one said anything. What could they say, anyway? The moment it came out, I regretted it. I felt like a scarlet letter had been placed on my blouse. I would be forever judged by these women and maybe their spouses too, or anyone else they told. My secret was out, as if no one had guessed it already.

After the episode at the cookout, I had distanced myself emotionally from most of my church friends. My mood was low and my anxiety was high. The last thing that I wanted was to surround myself with happily married couples. I felt like an outsider with them. As kind as they were, they could not relate to me. I stopped attending most social activities at church and withdrew from some volunteer positions.

Throughout my life, I'd excelled at distancing myself from others. I did it without trying and often without intending to. Whenever I felt threatened, smothered, inferior, or sad, my behavior would change. I would do things or say things to keep others away.

When you are depressed or anxious, your perception of reality becomes skewed. You don't think your behavior matters to anyone because you don't feel you matter. It's like a thick haze surrounds you and you can't see beyond it. All you can see is your own insignificant self. I lost many opportunities for friendship because of my tendency to push people away, but I am so thankful for the kind friends and family that stuck with me even when I pushed them away. They regularly called to check on us to make sure we were all right, and I can't imagine getting through this time without them.

I was alone, angry at the world and angry at God, and sinking even deeper into the hole I had been in for years.

Above me was darkness, and I could see no light and no way out of the pit I was stuck in. My weight was at an all-time low. I did my best to be a good mom to my boys, but I was deteriorating. Trying to overcompensate for my inner turmoil, I put extra effort into homeschooling. We continued to attend church even on the days I wanted to stay home, and I prayed continually for guidance.

Although I felt strange whenever I saw those women at the Bible study, I gradually began to feel a sense of relief for admitting my weakness. My struggle with anxiety and depression was something that I'd kept mostly to myself. I didn't tell strangers I was broken.

Even though I felt somewhat liberated through admitting my depression and anxiety to the ladies in our group, the study was a struggle. The book we were using was a source of frustration. Through her writing, the author implied that choice was involved with issues like anxiety and depression. When I first read this implication, I was outraged. What did she mean that I had a choice? I didn't have a choice. I was damaged. I was ill. I had a diagnosis! How dare this person insinuate that I could control my situation! Why would anyone choose to be this way?

Although I resented the book, I continued attending the Bible study. Quitting was out of the question. I didn't quit things. So I kept going. It was during this time, and the months to follow, that God slowly showed me a new reality.

Maybe I did have a choice. Maybe I had chosen to accept that I was broken and that I required a life of counseling and medication. Maybe I had accepted the idea that I would never get better. After all, I was sick.

Wasn't I?

Though the antidepressants were ineffective and my progress in counseling had stalled, I had my diagnosis. I had my label. Maybe I had become so accustomed to being an anxious and depressed grieving widow that I thought nothing else was possible. Maybe, on some level, I didn't want anything else to be possible. Perhaps I was still punishing myself.

As much as I knew in my head that God was in control, I had been the one responsible for caring for my husband. He died on my watch. Never mind that I had an infant and a two-year-old to care for, and a dog, and a house, and everything else, I should have been able to save him. It was my job as his caretaker to keep him alive, and I had failed. Part of me still held on to guilt that should have never been mine to hold. I was still punishing myself for something that I had no control over.

As I looked to Scripture for answers, I found them there waiting for me. I learned about joy, contentment, and peace. Although I had read the verses before, they suddenly made sense. God offers these blessings to all believers, but I had to choose to accept them. By living with a defeated mindset, full of guilt and sadness, I was denying them.

For years, pursuing anything that might bring me happiness had felt wrong, like I was insulting Rob's memory by interrupting my sadness. As ridiculous as it may sound, I felt shame when I enjoyed myself. Joy was something that I didn't think could ever be possible. What joy could there be for someone as broken as me?

Once I realized I had been punishing myself for years and that God had a plan for my life, I embraced a new reality, a reality of choices. I had to make some tough choices if I was ever going to improve my state of mind and experience joy. Was I going to let myself slip away, or was I going to do something about it?

I am not implying that I could just choose to have a healthy state of mind and that would miraculously solve my mental health issues. Rather, I needed to choose to stop living as a victim of my circumstances and become an active participant in my recovery instead of a passive bystander.

Eliminating the medications I had become dependent on became a priority. Even if it meant gaining weight and facing unknown challenges, I had to do it. But how?

CHAPTER 33

Escaping the System

Sitting in the nurse's office, I was prepared for my interrogation. I knew what questions she would ask since I had been through it so many times before. How are you feeling? Are you getting out and socializing? Are you active? The list went on, but I knew how to answer if I was well, and I wanted to be well. This was the first time I wholeheartedly wanted to be well and actually thought it was a possibility. In the past when I had been asked the questions, I always answered in a way that would show just how damaged I thought I was, thus ensuring the proper diagnosis of depression. I had been attached to that diagnosis, but now I wanted it gone.

Years earlier, when my counselor had moved locations to open her own practice, I went with her. Since the previous practice had required patients to receive counseling from someone at their location, moving with my counselor meant changing psychiatrists, again. This time, though, instead of a psychiatrist, I saw a nurse who could prescribe medications. When I first met her, she didn't seem certain that medication was the answer, but she gave it to me anyway.

At subsequent meetings, she would ask me the same series of questions and then ask how I was doing with my medications. I remember more than once she said something like "maybe this is just how you are," meaning that there wasn't anything inherently wrong with me that required medication. This used to bother me because I didn't want to be who I was. I didn't like who I was. Medication was supposed to make me someone else, someone better.

The reality was that the only medicines that had been even slightly effective in my many years of treatment had been the stimulant and the depressant. The various antidepressants were ineffective at treating my depression. Even though it probably caused my weight loss, the stimulant had helped with my energy level, and I liked the boost it gave me.

The depressant I was taking for anxiety had become a crutch. I was only taking a small dose, but I could pop a pill whenever I felt tense and it would almost immediately calm me down. It was a quick and easy fix, and taking it at night allowed me to relax enough to fall sleep.

Now, though, I felt like God was leading me in a new direction. I no longer felt that medication was the answer and that the time had come to stop taking it. The medication would not bring my husband back, and it would never take my sadness away. I realized I had been trapped in a system based on dependency for years. If I ever wanted to escape the system, I had to make some changes. Convinced I was permanently damaged, I thought I needed medication and continual counseling. What I needed was to trust that God would take care of me and show me ways to manage my symptoms without popping a pill.

For some, medication is a lifesaver and absolutely in their best interest, and I am not suggesting that anyone stop taking their medication without consulting a doctor. However, I feel that medication is not always the best choice at all times. When Rob was sick, the depressant that I took helped to keep my anxiety level down. As a result, I was better able to care for him and the boys. It was what I needed then.

However, over the years that followed Rob's death, medication cunningly became a way to avoid taking responsibility for myself and becoming the woman that God wanted me to be. I was believing the lie that I was permanently damaged and that I needed medication to live with my brokenness.

Sitting in the nurse's office, I answered her questions as convincingly as I could. Then I asked about stopping my medications. Secretly, I had already been decreasing my medications a little at a time. From all my years of different doctors and trying different antidepressants, I knew that you had to taper the dosage to avoid side effects. Having suffered those side effects in the past, I knew that doctors sometimes suggested a plan that tapered too quickly. So to make certain that I would be prescribed enough medicine to taper slowly, I had already been tapering my medicines. My nurse prescribed a plan to taper and then stop the medications as long as I kept seeing my counselor. I agreed and left with no intention of returning ever again.

Weeks later I found myself medication-free for the first time in years. However, I chose not to mention it to my counselor right away. I was afraid to say anything since she had encouraged medication. By this time our sessions had gone from weekly to biweekly and had become so much of a routine that I could predict what she would say each time. The same questions would be asked; the same suggestions would be made. Counseling was no longer as helpful as it once had been. I was at a point where the only way to move forward was to take a step on my own.

There was a time when counseling was absolutely necessary. I needed the accountability, and I needed the help that my therapist provided for me and my boys. Now I had grown, and the only way that I would continue to grow was to stop thinking of myself as a victim of my circumstances. I needed to act. I had to take responsibility for my health and my behavior.

Eventually, I confessed to my counselor I was no longer taking medication. I might have hurt her feelings by not telling her sooner, but I was a bit of a coward. I had been in a state of dependency for years, and I was fearful of going back. It wasn't long before our meetings went to monthly and then to "call if you need to come in." I don't remember exactly when it ended, but after years of counseling and medication, I was on my own. Of course, God was with me.

CHAPTER 34

Selling My Security

It didn't hit me until the first snowstorm occurred after selling my second rental property, just how trapped I had felt for so many years and what a strain the rental properties had put on us. For once, the only property I had to worry about was my own. I could just relax and watch the snow pile up if I wanted to. No one else was depending on me except my boys. I was finally free of a burden that I had no business taking on in the first place.

To say that Rob had been an ambitious guy would be an understatement. He'd been hardworking, driven, and motivated. At one time, he had visions of owning many rental properties, but only got so far as purchasing two. One was the property we had lived in for a brief time years before while unmarried, and the other was one he had purchased later. He took care of the properties and dealt with the tenants mostly on his own. I assisted as more of a support person with clerical tasks. The rentals were his thing, and I was fine with that. I didn't want that job.

After Rob died, the rentals were my responsibility. This became crystal clear to me at the wake when some tenants kindly showed up to pay their respects. It was almost like the feeling you get when you step into an ice-cold shower: an instant shock to your system. I hadn't been thinking about the rental properties. Now, I had to deal with them, and I had no idea how.

Sadly, I didn't deal with them. At least, I didn't deal with them well. The thought of selling them felt overwhelming when Rob died and for many years afterward. How would I even go about that? It was too much to think about. Besides, I was emotionally attached to one property whether or not I wanted to admit to it. We had lived in that house in our "glory days" when we were young, when Rob was healthy. I still had boxes in the attic there, and Rob had left a basement and garage there full of stuff that I did not know how to tackle.

Mostly, I was afraid. How could I sell off a potential income source? Would I be able to make my savings last? Would it be enough? It would be a risk, and Rob was the risk taker, not me. Besides, they were his properties. It felt like a betrayal to even consider selling them.

Looking back now, selling would have saved me countless sleepless nights that came from the problems I encountered with the rentals later. At that time, I couldn't handle another change. I had just lost my husband, and I craved stability. My world was falling apart, and I couldn't let our finances fall apart too.

At first the rentals took care of themselves. The tenants paid their rents and took care of minor repair issues on their own. I found someone to plow the snow in the winters, and one tenant mowed the grass in the summers. As time went on though, the rentals became an enormous problem. Tenants paid their rents late, bounced checks, and sometimes did not pay at all. During our house construction, moving, weight loss, anxiety, and depression, I became disorganized. I did not keep updated records, and sometimes I didn't immediately realize when a rent payment was overdue. I did not know how much money I was making or how much I was spending on the properties. It was a mess.

Sometimes I realized what was happening and tried to deal with it. I sent reminder letters and eviction notices. I gave second chances multiple times and had different tenants owing me hundreds of dollars when they left. Some tenants damaged the property. Others left behind mounds, and I do mean mounds, of garbage that I had to pay to deal with. Of course, I was usually so glad that they'd left that I didn't think much about the costs involved.

There was an extremely high emotional cost, too, that went along with dealing with the renters. As if my anxiety wasn't high enough, dealing with the properties increased it tenfold. A few times I had to take tenants to court.

On one of those terrible days, a kind friend offered to accompany me, and another kind friend offered to watch the boys. I was a nervous wreck. Surely the Lord drove that day, even though I was in the driver's seat, because I was completely lost on the way there. My friend was likely worried about her safety and my sanity as I maneuvered through the one-way streets to find the courthouse. I had thought I knew how to get there. I was wrong. I wanted to turn around and just forget the whole thing. But how could I? I had initiated the court proceedings. I couldn't skip it.

These tenants had become a serious problem for everyone else in the building, and they needed to go. I felt like such a mean person through it all, making people move from the place that they called home. The court mediator set one tenant straight that day, which helped to put my mind more at ease. The tenant was protesting the eviction and said something like "Why do I have to go?" to which the mediator replied something like "It's not your house." He was right. It was not the tenant's house; it was mine. As awful as I felt forcing those tenants to leave, I had the rest of the tenants in the building to think about, and my own stress level. It had to be done.

Besides the loss of rent from nonpayment and vacancies and the cost to repair property damage, there were costs associated with paying professionals to repair heating systems, replace water heaters, replace roofing, and perform other maintenance tasks. Being skilled in several trades, Rob had always done these things himself. Now, I had to pay contractors to do them.

There was also the cost of insurance, real estate taxes, and various utility payments. Many bills were extreme because of careless and clueless tenants. Instead of making an income, most years I lost it. Owning the properties was costing me money. I had to take funds out of my savings to cover bills. It was ridiculous. Still, I was afraid to sell, Years went by with me dealing or not dealing with each rental catastrophe as it came.

Around the time of what I think was my third court case, and not long after my Bible study revelation, something happened that snapped me out of my delusion. Of all things, God used a chicken to change my mind.

Many years earlier I had become interested in homesteading and natural living. That had been a part of our original home-building dream when Rob and I purchased the property. I had gardened for years and wanted to live off the land in the future. Raising chickens had been part of the plan. When the boys and I were finally settled in our new home and beginning our homeschooling journey, I researched what it would take to raise chickens for eggs. Raising chickens would be a great learning opportunity for all of us.

As with everything else, the simple way was not good enough. We would not just buy a chicken coop; we would make one. I was sure this would save us money and provide a learning opportunity. The construction of our home left lots of random pieces of lumber that we could use, and we already had plenty of tools that had belonged to Rob. How hard could it be?

The boys and I built the walls and roof pieces of the chicken coop in our basement. The boys already knew how to hammer nails and use an electric drill from previous homeschool projects. I certainly wasn't a carpenter, but I taught them the skills that Rob had taught me and gave them several occasions for practice. It took many hours and a great deal of frustration to build the pieces, but we did it. Once we finished, my mom and stepdad helped us put the final structure together outside. It was a little tricky because the pieces were not quite square, but we made it work.

As for the birds, we would not just purchase young hens—we would raise chicks, and not just any ordinary chicks. We would get heritage breeds because I had learned through my research that they were becoming threatened. If we were going to get chicks, we might as well support their survival. Besides, it seemed to coincide with a more natural homestead.

So the boys helped decide which chicks to get, and I placed the order. It felt strange that I could order birds online, but it provided a fun memory for our family. Arriving in the early morning at the post office to pick up a small box full of chirping chicks is something we will never forget. At first the chicks lived in a large box inside the house with us. The boys named all the birds and quickly grew attached to them. Once the chicks were old enough, they lived outside.

In the early days of owning chickens, the boys enjoyed watching the birds grow and caring for them. Sometimes they tried to play games with them. One of my favorite videos is of the boys playing outside, making what they were calling "chicken stew." They had a big pot of muddy water to which they were adding grass and random plants they had picked. One stirred the pot as the other one added the ingredients. At first it seemed like they were making something for the chickens to eat. They often picked grass and clover to feed the chickens. Their chicken stew took on a different meaning when one of them picked up a chicken and stood it in the pot. To their dismay, the chicken jumped out.

Owning chickens added another responsibility to my plate that was already too full. Since I had read that the most natural way to keep chickens was to let them free range as much as possible, I often let them loose in the yard. The birds usually stayed together as they roamed and didn't stray far from our house. Their squawking would usually alert us if a predator was near, and we could rush outside to scare it away. Sadly, we were not always fast enough, and we had some losses to hawks, foxes, and coyotes. Although I wanted to do what was best for the chickens, my anxiety heightened having to listen for their squawking all the time.

One day, a bird went missing. This wasn't just any chicken—it was a favorite of the boys. Already on edge, having had a terrible week of dealing with the rental properties and everything else, I was in no condition to deal with more stress. Just because I had realized that there was more to life than misery didn't mean that everything got better instantly. My burden was still exceedingly heavy, and I was still struggling by trying to carry it alone.

I looked for the missing chicken. It would be dusk soon, and the flock would head back into their house for the night. I checked all over the yard but couldn't find her. I enlisted the boys' help. Where was she? Refusing to accept the worst, I sent the boys back into the house and stayed outside and waited, and waited, and waited some more.

As I stood there, I was overcome with emotion. The thought of losing this chicken was the tipping point for my stress level. I could not handle another blow. I cried out to God. In tears, I let it all out. I sank to my knees in the middle of our stone driveway and prayed aloud. He knew my heart, but I told him anyway. I felt overwhelmed with my responsibilities. I couldn't take care of everything by myself. I was failing, and to add to my failures, our chicken was probably dead. What did God want me to do? Why did He open my eyes through the Bible study and then leave me alone to deal with my mess? What changes was I supposed to make? How could I move forward?

Making decisions alone was excruciating. I wanted to be rid of the rental properties but wasn't sure if I should sell them. What if it was a financial mistake? How would I provide for the boys? Would I have to go back to working full time?

On my knees with tears running down my face, I pleaded with God to show me a sign. I knew I wasn't supposed to need a sign, that I was supposed to just trust his plan, but I was desperate. If I should sell the properties and concentrate on the home front, then I asked him to show me something to confirm that, anything.

After a few minutes, I looked up and there was our missing chicken casually making her way across the yard. It was at that moment that my decision was made. I would sell the rental properties.

Sadly, selling the first house was a nightmare. In my eagerness to get rid of the property, I allowed myself to get swayed by a persuasive real estate agent against my better judgment and list the house before it was ready. The house was a mess. There were still tenants in one unit, and the house and surrounding property were littered with garbage. Listing the property then was a mistake. The rent-paying tenants ended up leaving, and I was left with a vacant house and less income.

Soon after the tenants moved out, someone broke into the house and stole the copper pipes. I remember the morning when we went to the house intending to fill a dumpster, only to find out that someone had broken a window and accessed the basement. I didn't even notice at first because the basement door was untouched and secured. We walked in not expecting anything other than cobwebs.

Within minutes I realized someone had cut and removed the copper. There I was standing in a scary dirty basement with my two young kids beside me, wondering whether the thieves were still in the house. I piled the kids into my car and called the police. My youngest was traumatized by that experience. For years after, he worried that someone would break into our home.

Things didn't get much better after the theft. The real estate agents were pushy, and I didn't think they were looking out for my best interests. The only bright side was that several months later I rented one unit to our new pastor and his family for a short while. Our longtime pastor had retired, and our interim pastor was leaving. Our church had hired a new pastor from out of state. He and his family were moving here and needed a place to stay.

Even though I felt a nudge on my heart, I didn't want to volunteer my property as a rental option for the pastor and his family. I didn't want to get involved. Sure, it may have been useful, but I was trying to sell it. Besides, it wasn't very nice. The major repairs were complete, but I was still emptying the attic and doing the cleaning as I was able. Interestingly, the more I tried to ignore the nudge, the stronger it became. So I prayed for guidance and felt led to tell someone at church that I had an empty place. I explained that the house was for sale. I wasn't expecting anything to come from it, but I felt relieved I had done my duty. The Lord had other plans.

For some strange reason, the people involved with helping the pastor find housing seemed to think my place was a good option. The remarkable people at our church pitched in to paint and clean up the apartment. This all happened with little involvement from me, and the family moved in shortly afterward. It was all odd. I didn't know what was going on with my own house, and I felt a new sense of awkwardness at church.

Regrettably, throughout this time I was still under contract with the real estate agency to sell the house. I wanted to take it off the market, but I was stuck. The pastor's family was only looking for an apartment until they could buy a home, so they were agreeable to living in a rental property that was for sale. Regretfully, they had to deal with showings and the pushy real estate agent. I think it may have hastened their home-buying process, because they didn't stay long. I felt terrible about that. The whole situation created an uneasiness with some folks at my church. I wished I had said nothing about having an empty house.

Around the time that the pastor found a house, I was presented with an offer from a potential buyer. Within a week, that offer fell through. My contract period with the agency ended shortly afterward, so I took the house off the market and rented it again. Fortunately, the new tenants worked out well and stayed for quite some time. It wasn't until I had an empty unit again that I tried to sell it for the second time. This time I chose a different real estate agency, and the house sold quickly.

Now I just had one rental property to deal with. I kept that one for a few more years until the potential cost of repairing it seemed too extreme to pay. I had good long-term tenants then, and I felt bad about selling, but I had to do it. I did not want to be a landlord anymore, and the house was not profitable. It had become a liability. I wanted to be free of that responsibility.

For years, I had been on the edge of my seat worrying about the properties. During every snowstorm and now every rainstorm, due to a leaky roof, I worried about the rentals. Over the years I had dragged the kids along with me countless times within a moment's notice to deal with random rental emergencies. We were all tired of it.

Thankfully, the second house sold. It took a little time, but it sold at a decent price. I was finally free of that burden. I was no longer a landlord.

Now what would I to do? What had I done? I had gotten rid of our source of income. I'd sold our security. That fear would revisit me again and again. Often it would come after speaking to someone else who would ask me what I planned to do. Our situation made little sense to others. How could I sell the rental properties and not have a job? Each time I would explain that we could survive on the proceeds from the house sales for a considerable amount of time, at least long enough to finish homeschooling. It would be fine.

Deep down, I worried. What if my budget was wrong? What if my investments lost value? Plus, I felt I "should" have a job because that was what society said.

Still, I did all I could to save money and avoid unnecessary expenses. I planted a garden each year so we would have low-cost organic produce, and I researched ways to avoid overspending.

When the dryer stopped working though, I naively called a repair person. I realized later that calling him had been a mistake when he told me the cost of the parts needed to repair it and recommended that I purchase a new machine instead. So I paid for a service call for nothing. Frustrated, I did some online research. I not only found the parts at a fraction of the quoted cost, but I also found several videos that showed how to install them. Indignant, I decided we would repair it ourselves. When the parts arrived, my oldest son and I took the machine apart and, with the help of the videos, performed the repair. It was challenging, but we fixed it and saved hundreds of dollars.

It was times like these, when we fixed the clothes dryer or when God presented another cost-saving opportunity, that I felt reassured we would be all right financially. I didn't need a job to prove anything to anyone. I could relax and seize moments as they came, like during that first snowstorm after I sold the second rental property. At that moment, I was beyond relieved that I was no longer a landlord. I relaxed in my new freedom and shared the experience of that blessing with the boys. We were all thankful that our real estate days were finally behind us and that the Lord had carried us through it all.

CHAPTER 35

Leaving Our Church

One morning at church, the sermon topic was about deciding when it was right to leave a church. I think the pastor meant it to discourage people from leaving. Ironically, to me it only reinforced the idea that we should consider it.

Our church had seen many changes since our longtime pastor had retired years earlier. Some changes were good, and some were not so good. Many people left and moved on to other churches, but not us. No, being stubborn, I was determined to stay even though many of our friends had gone. This was my church, our church. This was the place where Rob and I had found a new way of life together. This was the place where I had accepted Jesus as my savior. This was the place where my children had grown up in Sunday school. This was the place where our former pastor's wife had graciously organized a mom's Bible study so we could help each other grow in Christ. That group had led to friendships and support when I was first widowed. This was the place where people knew us and knew our history, at least some of it. This was the place where I volunteered in various capacities, serving the Lord in whatever ways I could, and this was the place where my children were involved in several programs. We were comfortable in this church, with these people. At least, we had been comfortable for a long time.

I can't say exactly when it happened, because it came on so slowly. It was a feeling that something wasn't right. Changes happened that made no sense to me. Words were spoken that scratched at my spirit. I felt uneasy when I went to church and questioned whether I was still being fed spiritually. I no longer felt like I was growing in my faith while at church and was just going through the motions. I was determined to stay, though, for the sake of my boys. They were still growing spiritually, or at least I hoped so, alongside their church friends.

On my own, I still made time for personal devotions. I read my Bible and prayed. The boys and I were completing a Bible study together as part of their schooling. I was learning more from that study than from anything else. At church, something was wrong.

I held out for the longest time. We would not leave. This was our church, and we were staying. My boys were comfortable and engaged. We would stay, if only for their sakes. Maybe it would get better. But that morning, I think the Lord used the sermon to place thoughts of doubt in my mind. Maybe we should leave.

A little later, the next trigger came. I remember the sick feeling in my stomach when it was announced without warning that Sunday school and another children's program were being eliminated. The two things that my kids were actively involved in were canceled. The two things that kept us coming back each week were gone.

Upset does not even begin to describe my feeling. I was devastated. I knew a church should not be about its programs. That's not why you go to church. However, these two things had become the only strings still pulling us to our church. It was almost like the Lord said, "I've cut those strings. What are you going to do now?"

We might have skipped church the following Sunday. We began skipping many Sundays. The boys were happy with skipping church, but they weren't entirely sure about leaving altogether and going somewhere new. I prayed continually for direction and sought counsel from trusted Christian friends who attended other churches. Leaving the church would be a big step, and I didn't know if I could do it.

I was surprised that no one checked on us when we first began missing church. We had been regulars for many years, barely missing a service. I suppose that only confirmed my decision to leave. Our church had become a stranger.

Trusting that the Lord was leading, I set out to find us a new church. The boys were not keen about going somewhere new, and I was anxious about it, but it had to be done. Going to church was important for our family, and we needed to be there. The first two churches that we attended were not a good fit. The Lord made that clear. None of us felt at ease. We tried one a second time, but it was worse than the first time.

For a while, we just didn't go to church at all. This was a tough time, even though I think the boys enjoyed staying home on Sundays. I would watch a sermon on television and go on with my day. However, I knew we were treading on a slippery slope. We needed to find a church, and we needed to do it soon. If we allowed ourselves to become too comfortable not going, we might never go back.

    I scoured the internet looking at church websites. I asked others where they attended. Then I prayed a deliberate prayer. Instead of asking, "Lord, please show me the way," I prayed, "Lord, please have someone invite us to church." Before long, that was exactly what happened, and we went. In that church, I found a loving Christian fellowship so like the one I'd first encountered years earlier with Rob at those evening services that I immediately felt at ease. God had answered my prayer and led us to our new church.

CHAPTER 36

The Forty-Dollar Salad

Sipping a cup of tea and chatting with a friend in her living room while our kids played upstairs, I was toying with an idea. Somehow the conversation had shifted to vacations and Walt Disney World in particular.

We had conversed about this topic before, but this time was different. My friend had traveled to Florida and visited the parks many times and enjoyed talking about it. Her enthusiasm was catchy, and I would often let myself to fantasize about a future trip that I had no real intention of taking.

Visiting Walt Disney World with the boys had long been a dream of mine. I had even deliberately charged everything that I could during the house construction to my Disney Visa® credit card to earn points for a trip. I would use the card for my spending and then just pay off the balance each month. I racked up tons of points this way. Regretfully, I did not fully understand the program and lost most of the points because of expiration dates. Now that I understood the program, I had just over five hundred dollars of "free Disney money" and no plan for how to spend it.

Until this day, I had not taken my dream vacation seriously. I had brainwashed myself into thinking trips were wasteful and that I didn't want to travel. Even so, there was a part of me that did. As a young adult, I'd enjoyed trips, and Walt Disney World had been one of my destinations. Rob and I had enjoyed traveling and exploring places together. That part of my life died with Rob, and I had convinced myself that it was better that way.

In reality, I was just plain scared to go anywhere, and I was doubly afraid to take the boys. Even if I wanted to take the boys to Walt Disney World, I didn't think I could handle them by myself. Various scenarios played out in my mind. What if they needed to go to the bathroom? I didn't know about family bathrooms. What if they got lost? They were not prone to wander, so I don't know why this worried me. What if they refused to participate when we got there? This was a legitimate concern, as it had happened several times before with homeschool outings. The more that I wanted them to join in, the more they refused. Sometimes they could be frustratingly difficult. So over the years, every time I had thought about my dream vacation, I convinced myself that it was a bad idea.

However, the boys were older now. They could go into the men's room by themselves, or at least go in together. According to Disney, they were not even considered "kids" anymore and could wander the parks without an adult. So, what was stopping me from booking a trip? It was a combination of fear and guilt. The fear was mostly because I had never done anything like this and didn't know what to expect. The guilt was based on the idea that I was being wasteful with our finances. Yet I had the free Disney money and had recently been hired to write an online math class. It wasn't much pay, but it was something. Besides, the kids had grown so fast. The days of dressing up as Woody and Buzz from Disney's *Toy Story* were long gone, and playing with toys wore thin by the day. It was now or never.

So as we sat and discussed all things Disney while enjoying our tea, my friend did some flight and hotel searches to price things out for me. I had not researched the actual cost before and was surprised to learn that it was less than I had imagined. Maybe we could go. On the ride home that day, my mind spun. Could we go? How would I tell the kids? I had sometimes hinted about going on vacation, and they had always been adamant about not going anywhere. They were homebodies and just as anxious as me about unfamiliar places and experiences, probably even more so.

Over the next few days, my excitement about the possibility of a trip to Disney didn't wane as it had in the past. A vacation would be a great way to make some memories with my boys before they were grown up. The timing felt right. Luke had been asking for a puppy off and on since the death of our beloved Mandy two years earlier. We could go on vacation and then look into adopting a dog. Maybe I could even use the promise of a puppy to help convince the boys to go.

Even though I was fearful of potentially doing something that seemed so out of bounds for us, I made a decision. We were going.

I chose to take a slow and steady approach with the boys, mentioning the possibility of a trip every so often, hoping they would come around and maybe even want to go. That didn't happen. Eventually, I had to just tell them I wanted us to go and that I would book the trip. At first, I don't think they took me seriously. They didn't want to go, and that was the end of it in their minds. I tried my best to get them excited about the trip, but they refused to express anything other than unhappiness.

As I planned our Disney vacation, I learned that I had a lot to learn. Reading websites, discussion boards, and books, as well as listening to podcasts, became almost a part-time job. As with everything else, I wanted to do it right. Even when I wasn't actively planning, I was still thinking about it. A combination of anxiety and excitement lingered in my body in the months leading up to our trip. I researched repeatedly how to save money on the trip. Even though I had decided it was all right for us to go, I was still determined to do it as inexpensively as possible.

Before long I knew which hotel to stay at, which tickets to buy, and which attractions to visit. I made touring plans and packing lists. I even began an exercise routine of walking to get my legs ready, and covertly increased the boys' exercise with additional active games. We all needed to prepare for the walking required at Walt Disney World. Then it was time to go. I said many prayers leading up to the trip, with many more to come.

Looking back now, the early morning flight was probably a poor choice, as was the airline that only offered open seating. I should have done more research in this area. We arrived at the airport with time to spare, even though my oldest had initially refused to leave his bed and it had taken a stern word from my mother to get him moving. My mom had graciously offered to transport us to and from the airport and take care of the home front while we were away. If it wasn't for her, we would probably not have gone at all.

Waiting to board the plane, the boys were remarkably calm. I tried to control my anxiety. Maybe it would be fine. We just had to get on the plane and sit together. I had confirmed our flight at the earliest moment allowed, exactly twenty-four hours prior. Surely that would enable us to sit together. Boy, was I wrong! Squeezing through the aisle, my eyes frantically searched the plane. I had instructed the kids that we would grab the first open row of three seats that we found. We walked until we reached the back of the plane. There were no open rows.

At that moment, I wanted to turn around and get off the plane, but with people pushing in behind us, there was no way to do it. Panic set in as the flight attendant sternly instructed everyone to choose a seat quickly. *No, I can't do it. This is my kids' first-ever flight. I have to sit with them.* I felt helpless. Our only option was the last row. There were two open seats on one side and a middle seat on the opposite side. That was the best we could do, and I tried my hardest to ignore the look of fear on the boys' faces.

The boys sat together, and I looked over at them repeatedly, trying to comfort them with my facial expressions. This was not the way I wanted to start the trip. Why had I been such a penny pincher? I'd known there was an option to pay for an early check-in that could have helped our boarding positions, but I had chosen not to pay it. I should have just paid for it or done more research and chosen a different airline that allowed for seat selection. Why did I think this would work out for us? This was a once-in-a-lifetime experience, and now it was spoiled. There was nothing I could do but try to stay calm.

As we lifted off, the boys were settled into playing games on their electronic devices. Every few minutes I leaned forward so I could see them. I likely annoyed the man next to me, but he never once offered me his aisle seat. From an outsider's point of view, my kids probably seemed old enough to sit alone, and flying on a plane should have been no big deal. In my mind though, these were my little boys, and I was an awful mother for dragging them on a plane to go somewhere that they didn't even want to go and then forcing them to sit apart from me.

Mostly, I felt cheated that I didn't get to experience the boy's first-ever flight with them. I wanted to know their thoughts. Were they scared? Were they excited? Did they have questions? I had not prepped them since they didn't enjoy discussing the trip. My guilt only multiplied when the flight attendant came around offering snacks and drinks. I had not told the kids about that part. Since they didn't know what to do, they refused them. This just added to my guilt. I took some solace in the fact that I could probably add the early check-in option to our flight home. I would pay the money, and it would be different next time.

Arriving at the airport in Orlando and finding our way to where we needed to be was easy. The chaos we soon found ourselves in, however, was not. We became part of a swarm of people, all attempting to get in line for transportation to the Disney resorts. This was not what I was expecting. I'd naively thought the mass of people must have been waiting for something else and foolishly attempted to walk past them all, only to realize that we had to join them.

This was our first of many magical crowds that we would find ourselves in on our trip. This was strike two. First, we couldn't sit together on the plane, and now we had to wait in a long line in a cramped area. Being slightly claustrophobic, this was not pleasant. Hiding my frustration was not something I did well. Sometimes I wished I was one of those people who could put on a fake smiling face, but that was not me. I tried for the sake of my boys to keep it in, but they could tell that I was bothered. What was supposed to be a once-in-a-lifetime magical trip was not turning out that way. I couldn't get upset though. If I got upset, the boys would get upset, and they hadn't even wanted to come in the first place. I needed to keep it together.

Strike three, or at least a foul ball, came when we got to the resort. I had received a text that our room was ready. I knew from listening to Disney planning podcasts that we should have been able to just go to our room, since it was ready, and avoid going to the front desk. But the magical bus driver instructed us to go to the desk.

Doing as we were told, we waited in another long line for our turn to check-in. Although the cast member, as the employees were called, was pleasant enough, the process irritated me, and I was cranky. I had to give her a ton of information they already had, like my cell phone number, which they had already texted. All I kept thinking was, *Why are you asking me this? You have this information.*

Finally we made it to our room and sat down. It was a pleasant space, but a little tight. After a few minutes, I unpacked and suggested that the boys do the same. Since

The Forty-Dollar Salad

I had a planned agenda for our day, we only had a set amount of time to stay at the resort. We needed to get to a park by a certain time to keep to our schedule.

All at once, the tears fell. I looked over, and both boys were crying. I think the realization that we would spend the next five nights in this little room away from home had suddenly sunk in and overwhelmed them. I felt their pain. It had been a lot to ask. We had done nothing like this before. It was at that moment that I abandoned my plan. My priority had to be getting the kids comfortable if we were going to have any enjoyment at all.

So even though I had meticulously planned and reserved our Fast Passes, Disney's advance ride reservation system, I decided that we would not go to the park as planned. Instead, we would get some food and unwind at the resort. Purchasing a pizza was the first step in a more positive direction. After eating, we spent some time at a playground near our room. Even though the boys had outgrown playgrounds at home, they enjoyed this one. No one else was there, and we all relaxed in peace. Smiles were plentiful as we enjoyed hanging out together. Maybe it would be all right after all.

Eventually we made our way to a park. We rode some rides and enjoyed new sights. We even arrived for our dinner reservation on time. This was when I got a proper sense of dining prices. The pizza we'd had earlier was reasonably priced, but I'd purchased that at the resort's food court. This was a restaurant in a park.

By the time the hostess seated us, I was so happy just to be there that I wasn't paying attention to prices. My only concern was whether there was something on the menu that the kids would eat. I had spent hours scouring menus to choose restaurants I thought would work well for us. When the server came and we worked out that Luke could order something from the kids' menu even though he was technically too old, and Noah had chosen something from the adult's menu, I chose the special of the day since it sounded good when the server said it, a grilled salmon salad. The server may have mentioned the price, but I didn't hear it.

I was too excited to think about prices. This was our first sit-down restaurant meal on our first vacation, and it was special. Besides, our Disney money from my credit card rewards was paying for our food. That was how I chose to use my rewards so we could eat without worrying about the cost. Good thing too, because when the bill arrived, I gasped. My salad cost more than the two boys' meals put together!

I don't know if it really was a $40 salad, but over time, that was what we came to jokingly call it. Whenever I attempt to duplicate that salad at home, I tell the kids I'm making my $40 salad, and it amuses them. I don't regret that meal choice at all. It was delicious, and the fact that it became a part of our vacation story is priceless.

Although the rest of the trip was enjoyable, the boys did not engage as much as I had hoped. They often complained of being tired while walking around the parks and wanted to spend more time in our room at the resort. This frustrated me, but I did my best to hide it. After all, it was no minor miracle that we were even there. Maybe if I didn't push them too much, they would want to return someday so we could experience more of the parks.

Our vacation days passed quickly, and suddenly it was time to leave. I was ready to go and sad to go at the same time. I think the boys were just happy to leave. This time at the airport, the plane wasn't nearly as crowded. Even though on our arrival day I had paid to add an early check-in for our return flight, I don't think we even needed it. Trying not to worry that I had wasted money on something we didn't need, I focused on being thankful that we could sit together.

All in all, our first vacation was an excellent experience. We had many fun moments, even if my kids would not admit to it, and I'm glad we went. We made some special memories together, and that was all I wanted, anyway.

CHAPTER 37

Afraid to Run

I wasn't sure if I could do it. Puttering around the house, I was delaying the inevitable, the decision whether to go for a run outside. The treadmill would be easier, since I wouldn't have to leave the house and try something new. But as scared as I was, I wanted to try something new. It was time. As I put on my shoes and fitness belt, fully loaded with all the gear I thought I needed to run outside, I prayed for strength and courage.

With much hesitation, I said goodbye to the kids and went out of the door. This was the first time I would run alone on our street, and I was frightened. I didn't know if I was more afraid of the distance or of being alone on the road. They both weighed heavily on my mind as I jogged my way out of the driveway and onto the street. It wasn't that we lived in an unsafe area. We didn't. It was being alone, all alone, without the false security of a vehicle at my immediate disposal or a house to guard me against the world that made me uneasy.

Once on the road, I felt better. Looking around, I noticed minor details as I passed them. These were things

I had never seen while driving in my car, like random wildflowers or a decorative border of plants in someone's yard. My confidence slowly increased as I went. Before I knew it, my phone's fitness app told me that I had already run a mile. I was doing it! I was running down the road!

But something happened in my head somewhere between mile one and mile two, and my fear returned. I felt very helpless. Darkness clouded my thinking. What if something happened at home while I was gone? Sure, the boys were teenagers now and able to be left alone, but I was still worried. I was too far now to get back quickly if they needed me. Would they be all right?

What if something happened to me? I had run outside before, but that was at the park across from my mom's house, and I always let her know when I was there. If I went missing, she would know it, or if I was hurt, she wasn't far away. Now I was running on the open road by myself, and I had to go ten miles to stick with my training plan. As my head filled with random thoughts of fear and doubt, my legs ached and my breathing became labored. What was I thinking? Why did I even start running? Who did I think I was, anyway? I was over forty and way too old for this.

It had all begun out of seemingly nowhere. Two years after our Disney vacation, I was longing for another trip to Florida. Although our trip had been mostly fun, the boys' lack of enthusiasm had left me with a powerful desire for a do-over. Maybe if we did it differently, they would enjoy it more and develop an interest in travel. This time, besides Walt Disney World, we would go to Universal Studios and Sea World. Surely that would make the trip more appealing to the boys. I had it all figured out.

Since our first trip, I had learned a lot more about credit card points, travel rewards, and cost-cutting techniques and had even mapped out a plan to cover the entire cost of a future vacation. Once my plan was in place, I focused my spending on specific credit cards and gradually earned all the points and cash I needed to pay for the trip. After carefully choosing the dates based on projected crowd levels and cost, I made hotel reservations. Now all I had to do was convince the boys that another trip was a good idea. It was no use. They wanted no part of it, and there was no way to convince them otherwise.

So with the boys refusing to accept the vacation plan, my options were to force them to go and deal with the negative consequences, or give up the plan completely. At least, I thought those were my only options. Forcing them would have meant little enjoyment for all of us, and I didn't want to be the only one excited about our trip, again.

With much disappointment, I abandoned the vacation plan. Even though I had spent months researching and planning to save enough points, miles, and cash to pay for the entire thing, I let it go. Since I had been so excited about the possibility of traveling again and was looking forward to it, this decision sent my mood to a low place for weeks. I felt myself sinking. When you have a history of depression, sometimes it's difficult to bounce back from disappointments.

To stop thinking about the lost vacation, I quit listening to some of my regular podcasts, the Disney and Universal travel-related shows that had kept my trip enthusiasm alive for months. It felt like a slap in the face to listen to them now, and I didn't want to torture myself.

As I was deleting my favorites, I was torn about one of them. It was a light-hearted show that had always put a smile on my face, but it was Disney focused. Maybe, I thought, I would listen to just one more episode before getting rid of that show too. I put on my headphones, hit Play, and went for a walk with our two young dogs.

The podcast episode that day was about runDisney. Since I wasn't a runner and had little interest in the topic, I almost turned the podcast off. Running was not something I did or had considered doing. My sole source of exercise consisted of walking our two dogs, which we'd adopted as puppies after our vacation, up and down our long driveway. Instead of shutting off the podcast and looking for something else, I kept it on for old times' sake. As the jovial folks began speaking, I felt like a group of longtime friends had joined me on my walk.

Continuing along, I listened nonchalantly until a discussion ensued about how fun it is to combine a race with a Disney vacation. My ears perked up. I didn't know that people intentionally went to Walt Disney World to run a race and then stayed to visit the parks. Then they mentioned that many people do this solo. What? Solo?

As the podcast continued, I learned that there were free training plans available for beginner runners online. Not only that, but there were also communities of runners that supported each other. Beginning runners could follow a training plan, go to Walt Disney World, run a race, enjoy the parks, and do it solo.

Maybe I could go to Walt Disney World solo and take part in a race. Could I do that? The speakers mentioned that there were several races, each a different distance.

Maybe I could do a short race. Could I run a short race? Was I crazy to even consider it?

I had not run regularly since high school, when I took part in track and cross-country. Regrettably, I didn't like cross-country and usually felt defeated running long distances. Track was a little better, but I was slow and unambitious. My only other running activity had been brief bouts in my early twenties, but I never stuck with it and didn't enjoy it. Would I enjoy running now or like it enough to train for a race? Could I even physically do it? My body had gradually returned to a normal weight and stabilized after stopping the medications, but I was not in shape. Running seemed almost impossible, given my lack of fitness.

My heart pumped with excitement though, and my head swam as to listened to the show and considered the impossible possibility. Maybe I could go to Walt Disney World on my own and run a race. Was I brave enough for that?

After listening to that podcast, my mood lifted. I prayed for strength and guidance, knowing that the only way this would happen was if God made it so. I was not physically or mentally able to do it on my own. Even though I thought it was practically impossible, I also knew that nothing was impossible with God. If it was His will, then He could make it happen. Did I trust him enough to take a step forward in faith, even though I could fail miserably and make a fool of myself?

In the days that followed, I went into research mode to learn all that I could about the events and about running. I joined the online community mentioned in the podcast, and they gave me encouragement to get started.

Considering the different runDisney races, I decided on the Star Wars Half Marathon, which was a year away. Since I was not feeling confident that I could get myself in shape quickly, choosing this race would allow me plenty of time to train. I downloaded a training plan and began following it right away. It felt great to have a plan and something to focus on.

The first few weeks were hard. I walked more than I ran, but that was fine since I was doing the method of training that used walk breaks. Three times a week I was on my treadmill doing my prescribed training. I looked forward to writing a big check mark on my plan after I finished each workout. As the distances increased, the monotony of the treadmill became less desirable. That was when I began to run at the park across from my mom's house, but the trails there were limited. I needed to run longer distances to stick to my plan. I either had to run on the road or find trails elsewhere. Since there were no trails nearby, running on the road made the most sense.

So there I was, running down the road, overcome with doubts and not knowing what to do. Maybe I should just turn around and go home. What was I thinking, starting this journey? It was foolish. I couldn't do this. I wrestled with myself and prayed for strength again.

Then I changed what I was listening to on my headphones to something more upbeat. As I did, a switch inside me flipped and my attitude improved. No, I was not giving up. I had not begun this journey only to quit when it challenged me. Once I resolved to keep going, the miles got easier. God gave me the strength I needed. Before I knew it, I was back in my driveway having completed the ten miles I'd set out to do.

CHAPTER 38

Running Forward

In darkness, I left my house that morning to run my first 10k race. The boys had said their goodbyes and wished me good luck with sleepy smiles. Filled with excitement and anticipation, I began the almost two-hour drive to Narragansett, Rhode Island. Even the highway seemed like it was still sleeping with only a few cars on the road. It felt strange to be up and out so early on the weekend and even stranger to be on my way to run my third-ever race, and a second time racing with my friend.

Months earlier, I'd run a 5k race with her. She had been a runner for many years but hadn't raced in a while. That 5k race was to be a fun summer run, and that was exactly what it turned out to be. That was my second 5k race.

My first 5k, the first race since beginning this running journey, had been a few months earlier. I had been following my training plan carefully, and part of the plan was to complete a 5k race. This was all new to me, and I was scared.

Just deciding which race to choose was daunting. There was no shortage of 5k races within a reasonable driving distance, but I did not know which one to start with. I didn't want to choose a race that was too serious. I was running regularly, but not quickly. I wanted to be with other new runners, and I wanted my first race to be an enjoyable experience.

So I bravely registered for a charitable race at a nearby Christian school. My mom offered to come to the race and bring my boys so they could witness this momentous occasion. It was a lovely morning for a run, and I was ready. At least, I was ready after visiting the ladies' room three or four times. It's funny how nerves can affect you. It was a low-key race with lots of families taking part.

When I checked-in, the woman asked me why I had registered. I suspected that most of the participants were affiliated with the school somehow, and she was asking because I didn't look familiar to her. The question startled me. Should I tell her my story? "Well, you see, I've been through some struggles, and I just began running. I was trying to choose my first race, and your race seemed like a nice one." Instead, I just told her I had seen the race advertised online, which was true.

The start of the race was almost surreal. My mom and the boys wished me luck before I lined up with the other participants. Standing there felt strange. I looked around at the other runners and wondered whether I even belonged there. I knew I could run, or at least walk the distance, but would everyone pass me?

There were serious looking runners in front near the starting line. Surely they were here to compete. I wasn't. I just wanted to finish strong. This was a major step for me, registering for my first race in an unfamiliar setting with a bunch of strangers. It was no small feat for a shy introvert with anxiety issues. But God is bigger than that, and I knew it. He had carried me this far, and I was eager to see what He had in store for me with this race.

Since this event was for a Christian school, it began with prayer. What a wonderful way to begin my first race! The gun sounded, and a massive sprint ensued down the road. To not wear myself out early, I moved over to the side and ran at my normal pace. No way was I sprinting. Staying true to my training, I ran and walked in intervals. I had created a special playlist of upbeat music, and listening to it with my headphones kept me motivated. There was only one time that I almost lost my way, literally.

Before the race, I had reviewed the course map. My biggest fear was that I would get separated from the other runners and somehow deviate from the course. Surely, I had reasoned, the course would be well marked. This was not the case. One part of the course required runners to complete a loop, make a turn, and then complete another loop before traversing the same road again. When I reached the first loop, I knew that something was amiss. Runners coming from the turn area yelled to the volunteers for instructions. Some runners were not making the turn and instead were running down the road to the finish.

As I completed the loop, some runners ahead of me went straight instead of turning. I was confused. Which way was I supposed to go? Had the runners up ahead been in front of me the entire time, or had they come from somewhere else? I was fairly certain they had been in front of me. Why were they going straight?

Though young volunteers were standing in the road,

they weren't directing me as I ran toward them. They were not even paying attention. I considered my options. Should I just go straight and finish? I suspected that would have meant not completing the full distance. Or should I ask for help? I was tired. I could just run to the finish and be done. That was what my younger self would have done. I would have taken the easy road out and celebrated my good luck in finishing early. No one was paying attention, anyway.

But I wasn't that girl anymore. No, I was not cheating myself out of my first 5k! I came to run a full race, and I would do it right. So I asked a volunteer for directions and got myself back on track. I'm glad I did, because my mom and the boys were waiting on that last loop to cheer me on, and I would have missed them if I had gone the wrong way. It was such a treat to see them there supporting me.

The finish came fast after that, and they greeted me with a lovely bouquet of flowers. I felt amazing! I had completed my first race! This woman who had lost her husband, who had struggled with depression, anxiety, and various obstacles for years, who had been afraid to run down the road by herself, had just completed a 5k race and actually enjoyed it. Now I understood why folks took part in these events. It was fun!

As time passed on that dark drive to my first 10k, I prayed. This wasn't just any 10k. This was the race that I planned to use as my proof of time for my goal race, the runDisney half-marathon. There were so many participants in the Disney races that they grouped runners in corrals by speed and then staggered the start times. I didn't want to be in the last corral for fear of being swept. Runners must maintain a certain pace to remain in the race, and the farther up in the corrals, the better your chances of staying in the race. At least, according to my research.

So I had figured out what finish time I probably needed in this 10k race to be placed in an earlier corral at the half-marathon if I submitted it as my proof of time. My training had been focused on trying to achieve that time. That was part of my prayer. I asked for strength, an enjoyable race, and the target finish time. It may sound silly, but I prayed for two finish times. I wanted to go fast enough to be placed in an earlier corral, but I had my heart set on a better time. A time I wasn't sure I could achieve. An optimistic time, given my training.

After arriving at check-in, I picked up my bib and met my friend. Once we had boarded a bus that would drive us to the start line, I cast a long look at my surroundings. The sun was just rising over the ocean next to us. I could barely see the water when I had arrived, but there it was now, slowly appearing from the darkness. I looked forward to seeing it in all its splendor at the finish of the race.

As the bus departed, my friend remarked about the number of racers. Just like us, all those people had risen early to take part in this race. By far, this was the biggest race for me, with many racers. Each one had their own story, but they all had one thing in common—they all had chosen to get up early and run this race. It was almost unbelievable.

Less than a year earlier, I would never have imagined that my future self would be riding on a bus in the early morning hours to run a 10k race. It was a complete turnaround. Exercise used to be a chore. I did it occasionally because I felt like I should. Now, I ran because I wanted to run. Running made me feel strong, and I was so tired of feeling weak. Running improved my mood and calmed my mind. It was something I could do for myself to stay healthy. Being on that bus, surrounded by other runners, I felt even stronger. I was a runner.

With the sun fully risen, we departed the bus. Since it wasn't time yet for the race, my friend and I walked around to keep our legs warm and chatted about Disney. This friend would join me in a few months to run the half-marathon. Even though I was fully prepared to go on my running vacation solo, I had mentioned the trip to my friend, and she decided to run the race too. Unlike my prior vacation to Walt Disney World when I kept all the planning to myself because the boys didn't want to talk about it, now I could enthusiastically chat with my friend about our upcoming adventure.

As we lined up for the race, I was a little concerned about our starting position. We were supposed to be lining up by time, and my friend encouraged me to start next to her. Knowing she was a faster runner, I wasn't sure about that. The fear of being pushed along by the group of runners behind me at a too-fast pace filled me with anxiety. Nevertheless, I took some deep breaths and stood with my friend. Then we were off. That first mile was faster than I usually ran, and I was shocked at how good I felt. The miles that followed were a little slower, but I kept a good pace, all the while trying to appreciate every moment of it. This was the race that would bring me one step closer to my ultimate running goal and a magical vacation.

As I entered the final stretch, I could see my sister and my niece standing on the side of the road. It was a wonderful sight and gave me the push that I needed to finish the race. I was so touched and thrilled that they came to support me. Running over the finish line, I had no idea if I had met my goal since I forgot to stop the running app on my phone, and I wasn't wearing a watch. At that moment, it didn't matter. I had just finished my first 10k, and it felt great!

After enjoying the beautiful ocean view and dipping my toes into the chilly water, my sister and niece left, and my friend and I headed to a coffee shop. While we sat and chatted, a text message came with the race results. Without my reading glasses, I couldn't see the numbers. My friend searched the list of finishers, and my heart pounded with anticipation. I couldn't believe it when she read my finish time. It was the faster time that I had prayed for, exactly! God is amazing!

CHAPTER 39

A Beautiful Tomorrow

It was an unusual experience wandering around Magic Kingdom Park by myself. I had no responsibilities. I could go wherever I wanted and do whatever I wanted. It was marvelous, and I had not felt that way before. I was almost overwhelmed by the sensation of the utter relaxation and enjoyment that ran through me. My mom was taking care of everything back home, and the friend I had traveled with was enjoying some personal time of her own somewhere in the park. Unfamiliar with this level of freedom, I didn't know what to do with myself. The park was crowded with families going this way and that, but I hardly noticed.

After purchasing a coffee and a snack, I sat down to catch a glimpse of a show happening in front of Cinderella Castle. Feeling the sun cast its warm glow on my outstretched tired and achy legs felt amazing. It was just the day before that these legs crossed the finish line of the half-marathon. God had done it. He had allowed me to finish the race and finish it strong.

Even though I had been training for over a year, the race had still been challenging. Waking up at 2:00 a.m. to be on a bus by 3:30 a.m. to get to the race was difficult, especially since I had trouble sleeping that night. I attempted to fall asleep around 8:00 p.m., but a combination of noise and anxiety kept me awake. Even so, I was ready and eager to go that early morning. I had come all this way to do this special thing, and nothing would stop me.

At the race, my friend and I separated into our designated corrals near the starting line. It felt strange and lonely to be standing in the dark with a large group of strangers. My heart swelled when I received several text messages from folks back home wishing me luck. I was in awe that they were up so early and thinking of me. I felt loved and blessed to have their support.

I prayed repeatedly and asked for strength. Before I knew it, the fireworks lit up the sky, and it was my turn to run the race I had been thinking about for a year. The beginning was easy. I kept to my pace as the miles passed by. The on-course entertainment helped keep me motivated. I'm not sure when I noticed the humidity, but my body sure felt it. My heart rate was high, and my thirst was elevated. Even though I had brought water, I made use of and was thankful for the water stops along the course.

Running through Disney's Animal Kingdom Theme Park was incredible! Cast members cheered for us, and hearing them lifted the burden of the task. Nighttime faded, and the sun came up to greet us. I had never run through a sunrise before, and it was surreal, almost magical. Not long after, though, I felt hot and sluggish. The heart icon on my fitness watch flashed at me like a beacon, and the number it displayed as my heart rate was one I had never seen before in my runs. Usually, my heart rate had been consistent. I tried not to worry about it and kept going, being careful to stop for walk breaks regularly.

By the time I entered Epcot, the last leg, I was more than ready to stop. As I passed the different countries of World Showcase, I could hear the cast members cheering in different languages. It was fabulous! Yet I kept wondering how close I was to the finish. It seemed like it was taking forever.

Throughout the race, the mile markers did not match up with the miles tracking on my watch, so I did not know how much more I had to run. According to my watch, I should have been within viewing distance of the finish line, but I wasn't. The course went on and on. Finally, I heard someone yell out we were almost there, only a quarter of a mile more. A quarter-mile? I could do that. That was less than my driveway. With a newfound determination, I dug deep to pick up the pace.

My heart sank when I came into view of the big clock at the finish line. My goal had been to finish in under three hours, and the clock time was well over that. Even though I was wearing a running watch, I didn't think I could trust the time, since it had not been matching the course. I didn't know how I was doing. Had I been running over three hours already?

In training for the race, I had run fourteen miles in almost three hours. That was without humidity though, and I had not stopped. During this race, I had stopped for a photo opportunity and had also stopped for a bathroom break. Maybe I had been running for over three hours.

It's funny how many thoughts can go through your head in an instant. When I saw the clock, the disappointment of not meeting my goal played games with my mind. I wished I had told no one back home about wanting to finish in under three hours. I should have just kept that to myself. Now, they would be disappointed. Maybe I should just take it easy through the finish since I hadn't met my goal.

No, I would not dwell on it. I had come all this way to finish this race strong regardless of time. Completing the race was the actual goal, and I would give my best effort no matter what.

Maintaining my pace while attempting to control my breathing, I tried to smile as I pushed forward to the finish. Inside, I was smiling. Outside, my face was likely showing signs of the pain in my legs. Crossing the finish line, I couldn't comprehend what had just happened. Finally I could stop running. The time didn't matter. I had finished the race!

A year earlier, when I'd first began training, I had worried that I would not finish the race. I was afraid I would be too slow. Not only had I improved the past year, but I had improved enough to earn placement in a designated corral. This mom in her late forties who had lived through so much pain had just finished a half-marathon. It was beyond comprehension. Surely this was God's work.

Another blessing was yet to come when I finally realized that the clock time was not my time. In my running fog of confusion, I had forgotten that we had started in waves. The clock time started with the first wave of runners. My group had started several minutes afterward. That was why our bibs had timing chips. Duh! I was in awe when I found out my time: 2:54. I had finished

A Beautiful Tomorrow

in under three hours. That was a cherry on top of a very sweet cake.

Thinking back on the race as I sat enjoying my freedom at Magic Kingdom Park, my excitement level rose, and I had to move. With no destination in mind, I began walking. I remembered being at Walt Disney World with the boys several years before and wished they had come this time. I missed them, but I was completely at ease with myself for once. They had wanted to stay home, and I knew they were in excellent hands.

After strolling for some time and sitting down once more, I did something I had never done before. I decided to go on a ride by myself. This may not sound monumental, but it was for me. Walt Disney's Carousel of Progress is more of an attraction than a ride, but it was what I chose. Standing in line by myself felt strange with groups and families all around me. Once inside, my uneasiness left as I recollected the surroundings. The boys and I had done this ride. I wasn't sure if they'd enjoyed it as much as I did, but I had been looking forward to possibly doing it again on this trip.

As the ride music played and I listened to the lyrics telling me that there's a great big beautiful tomorrow, I realized how meaningful those words were at that moment. I had finally realized that there is a beautiful tomorrow waiting for me. How do I know? I know because of all the days that came before. I have walked along some very dark paths, and the Lord has never left me. He has always led me to a beautiful tomorrow. Each day brings its own blessings. We just need to open our eyes to see them. He continues to amaze me with all that He has allowed me to experience. Even in hardship, there were blessings.

Even in mourning, there was comfort. As written in Psalm 30:5 (ESV), "Weeping may tarry for the night, but joy comes with the morning." I can always look forward to the morning when I know that God is for me.

    Years earlier I didn't know that joy was waiting for me. I didn't know that I had to choose to accept it. I felt trapped in a state of brokenness and powerlessness. Now I knew that even on the days when I was at my lowest, I had a choice. I could stay in the lowly pit of doom, or I could reach out to Him and take comfort in knowing that He will show me a beautiful tomorrow.

CHAPTER 40

Freedom from Fairy Tales

Ending my story there, in Magic Kingdom Park, at the "happiest place on Earth," listening to the words that reassured my mind of the beautiful days to come, would be a lovely fairy tale ending to my story, but I no longer believe in fairy tales, and leaving you there would give a false impression of my reality. There was a time when I believed, as many young girls do, in magical happy endings. Now, I am free from the burden of that unrealistic story. It's not that I don't love happy endings and the wonder of imagination. I do. However, it is easy to get lost and become complacent in a false reality. Each day brings its own struggles, and pretending that's not the case helps no one.

Once I returned home from my trip, I settled into normalcy again. The boys and the dogs were happy to go back to their routines, and it felt nice to sleep in my own bed again. It didn't take long, though, for me to sink. It is probably common to feel downtrodden when you return to reality after a vacation. It is wonderful to get away for a little while and forget about your responsibilities, and I'm sure it's not unusual to experience some sadness when it's over, especially if you have planned for something and dreamed about it for a year.

However, when you have a history of depression and anxiety, emotions can sometimes escalate out of control. Instead of a little sadness, you can experience extreme gloom. I have had days in the past when I could barely function. What is different now, though, is that I have learned to recognize the warning signs. I don't think my issues will ever totally go away. They are part of me. However, I get to choose how I respond.

One lesson I have learned over the years is that a proactive approach works best for me. Even before I left on my trip, I suspected that I might have trouble when I returned. Therefore, I permitted myself to take it easy when I got home. This was fine for the first few days. When I tried to resume my full responsibilities, I struggled. Thankfully, I knew the signs. Irritability and grumpiness made their appearances first, and then tiredness set in. I had to draw the curtain on them fast and bring on the next act.

Years ago, when I was in counseling, my therapist gave me a brilliant tool. She had me think of several things that brought me happiness, and she wrote them on an index card. These were to be my secret weapons. Whenever I was feeling low, I was to look at the card, choose one thing, and do it. Taking action to help myself was key. I carried this index card in my purse for years. My secret weapons were simple things like listening to music. Music has almost always worked for me, especially if it is something upbeat that spurs movement. It's difficult to feel down when you're singing and dancing.

Often, when your mood is low, you don't naturally

think of ways to help yourself. You are so caught up in your sadness or anxiety that figuring out a way to get out of it does not even enter your mind. It's like you are standing frozen in a room of complete darkness. There is a light switch within reach, you know it's there, but it doesn't occur to you to touch it.

That index card and the others that followed later helped me countless times. The other interesting thing about those cards is that I could use them as a gauge. If I noticed I was feeling low, I could look at a card and determine whether I had done any of the items recently. The answer was always no. Then I would have the revelation that I was feeling poorly because I had neglected to do anything enjoyable. You would think having this revelation would be a onetime event, but no. It happened and continues to happen countless times. Logic does not enter into the depression equation. When you are depressed, you are depressed. When you are anxious, you are anxious. A little card with a few "try this" suggestions may sound silly, but actionable steps can be extremely helpful.

Running is another way to manage my mood. I can wake up irritable and down, but if I go for a run, I feel better afterward. Sometimes part of my brain tries to convince me that running is a bad idea, that I should just stay home. It's difficult to resist that lie, but I have learned to fight it. Deep down I know that running makes me feel stronger, not weaker. Inactivity only fuels depression and anxiety.

Sometimes even when you think you are better, bad habits reemerge. As the weeks went by after my trip and I returned to my regular running routine, I looked for a new challenge. Instead of just being happy with my accomplishment of finishing the half-marathon, and being content with running to stay healthy, I fixated on my speed, or lack thereof. Insecurity and doubt came for another visit and convinced me I wasn't good enough. I needed to run faster to be a real runner.

So I found a training plan that promised to improve my speed, and I began training for a 5K race. At first, everything was fine. The first few weeks were easy. Then the speed workouts became more challenging. Before long, I experienced a familiar pain in my right knee.

A few months after I had first started running, I experienced knee pain in both legs. This resulted in a reduced training load and weeks of physical therapy, but eventually the pain went away. The strength-building exercises that I had started back then had been a part of my routine ever since—that is, until a few weeks after I started the speed plan. Neglecting the exercises was my first mistake. Running while in pain was my second mistake.

Since I had experienced knee pain before, I thought it was nothing special and continued to follow the training plan. The pain worsened and caused me to alter my stride to favor my right side. Not following the plan was not an option. I was not a quitter. I had to follow the plan if I wanted to reach my new goal.

As I attempted to ignore my pain, another pain presented itself. This time it was my lower left leg, and it was not so easily ignored. The more that I tried to run, the worse the pain became. It got so bad that I was limping whenever I walked. With the 5K fast approaching, I finally admitted to myself that I needed a break.

After spending a week with no running, I felt restless. I waited a few more days and then went for what I thought would be an easy run. At first my legs felt great. As I went along, I thought maybe I could still meet my goal. The race was about two weeks away. Maybe I could do it. Just as I was thinking this, about a half mile into my run, I felt a zing of pain in my right knee. A few steps later, my left calf seized up, and my run was over. Staggering back home, I felt defeated, since I would not achieve my goal, and my stubbornness had been the cause.

Over the next two weeks, I rested, iced, compressed, and elevated my legs as much as possible and did not run. Not attempting the race was not an option. Weeks earlier I had convinced my running friend to do the race with me, and I was not backing out now even if I had to walk the course.

By race day, I did not know what would happen with my legs and feared that my calf would seize up again, causing me to drop out completely. My prayer leading up to the race was to complete it without pain. Thankfully, God answered that prayer. It turned out to be my slowest 5K, but I ran the entire way and was thrilled. It's amusingly ironic that I was training for my fastest race time, finished with my slowest race time, and was overjoyed.

Goals are great, but not if they stem from a place of shame or pride. Even though I am stronger and wiser than I was years ago, I can still fall victim to my insecurities when I forget that I am God's child and instead believe the lies that society constantly whispers.

Since experiencing that interesting dream many years ago about writing my testimony, I have faced many trials. These challenges have become part of my story. My testimony is not a onetime event. Every day the Lord shows me something new. I would never have imagined that running would become part of my story, and I am thankful for this addition to my life. Each run is a blessing and a reminder to keep moving forward.

Growing in the Lord over the years, I am not the same person today that I was when I first accepted Christ as my savior, nor am I exactly the same as I was yesterday. He has taught me many lessons, but the most surprising thing He has taught me is that He created me perfectly for His purposes, even if I never come to know what those purposes are. That does not mean that I am perfect, nor does it mean that I should strive toward perfection. I am quiet, shy, and socially awkward, and He designed me that way on purpose. I can let go of unrealistic worldly expectations and accept myself as I am, as God's perfect creation. He created me to be me, and He does not make mistakes.

Even though I have suffered much hardship and battled anxiety and depression, contrary to my former understanding, I am not defective or without worth. We are all broken in our own ways, but that does not mean we are useless. Brokenness is not an excuse to give up. We have value and purpose to Him. We must continue to move forward and to grow.

On the days I struggle, I am no longer stuck in the pit that once held me. I need not live my life as a victim. Instead, I can choose to latch on to joy and hope, but this is a choice that I must deliberately make and must make it regularly. There are days when I have to repeatedly remind myself about this choice, as it is so easy to slide backward. Sometimes I stray back to what could have been. My heart still aches for Rob, and this pain can lead me to a familiar dark place and a defeated mindset. But when I slip, I am not alone. God is there, and He is gently guiding me forward to fulfill the purpose He has for my life. My testimony exists in living for that purpose and faithfully following wherever He leads me.

A poem is where I feel led at this moment, and that is where I leave you. Thank you for reading my story. I wish you many blessings for your journey.

Beautifully Broken

Beautifully broken,
No place for shame,
Most perfectly imperfect,
God made me this way.

Designed for His purposes,
His blueprints unseen,
Trusting imperfections,
I see not what He sees.

In a world of illusions,
A mask I won't wear.
Awkwardness unavoidable,
The weight I must bear.

Beautifully broken,
Content in His plan,
A master's creation,
Sculpted by loving hands.

Thanks again for reading my story. I hope it has blessed you in some way. If you enjoyed reading *Looking Back and Running Forward*, please help others find this book by leaving a review where you purchased it. Thank you!

You can learn more about me and my writing, and subscribe to my monthly newsletter, by visiting the site heidikinney.com.

Follow me at:

facebook.com/HKinneyWriter

instagram.com/hkinneywriter

www.ingramcontent.com/pod-product-compliance
Lightning Source LLC
Chambersburg PA
CBHW020905080526
44589CB00011B/444